THE POWER OF GRAMMAR

THE POWER OF
GRAMMAR

Unconventional Approaches to the Conventions of Language

Mary Ehrenworth
Vicki Vinton

HEINEMANN
PORTSMOUTH, NH

Heinemann
A division of Reed Elsevier Inc.
361 Hanover Street
Portsmouth, NH 03801–3912
www.heinemann.com

Offices and agents throughout the world

The authors and publisher wish to thank those who have generously given permission to reprint borrowed material:

"Around the Corner" by Sharon Bryan was originally published in *In Short,* edited by Judith Kitchen and Mary Paumier Jones. Copyright © 1996 by Sharon Bryan. Reprinted by permission of the author.

"Getting Ready" from *Everything's a Verb* by Debra Marquart. Copyright © 1995 by Debra Marquart. Reprinted with the permission of New Rivers Press, *www.newriverspress.com.*

"In Praise of the Humble Comma" by Pico Iyer was published in *TIME,* June 13, 1988. Copyright © 1988 by TIME, Inc. Reprinted by permission.

"justice" by William Rodriguez was originally published in *The Party Train* edited by Robert Alexander, C. W. Truesdale, and Mark Vinz. Copyright © 1996. Reprinted by permission of the author.

Excerpt from *Woman Hollering Creek* by Sandra Cisneros. Copyright © 1991 by Sandra Cisneros. Published by Vintage Books, a division of Random House, Inc., and originally in hardcover by Random House, Inc. Reprinted by permission of Susan Bergholz Literary Services, New York. All rights reserved.

Library of Congress Cataloging-in-Publication Data
Ehrenworth, Mary.
    The power of grammar : unconventional approaches to the conventions of language /
Mary Ehrenworth and Vicki Vinton.
        p.   cm.
    Includes bibliographical references and index.
    ISBN 0-325-00688-1 (acid-free paper)
    1. English language—Grammar—Study and teaching.   2. English language—Rhetoric—Study and teaching.   3. English language—Composition and exercises—Study and teaching.
4. Report writing—Study and teaching.   I. Vinton, Vicki.   II. Title.

PE1404.E36 2005
428.2'071—dc22   2004025562

Editor: Kate Montgomery
Production: Lynne Costa
Cover design: Jenny Jensen Greenleaf
Typesetter: Publishers' Design and Production Services, Inc.
Manufacturing: Steve Bernier

Printed in the United States of America on acid-free paper
09   08   07   06   05   VP   3   4   5

Dedicated to
Kate Montgomery, editor extraordinaire,
whose wisdom, generosity, acumen, and faith
guided us through every page

Contents

content as these students conduct an inquiry, and we study the processes of class-room inquiry. We investigate the impact on student writing of this new knowledge and the implications for our understandings of grammar and for our teaching.

Chapter Five   127
The Sentence and the Apprentice
Chapter 5 presents student writers apprenticing themselves to published authors at the sentence level. We study how to read a sentence closely and parse it for meaning. We consider the internal forms of sentence construction. We see students experimenting with style, and we see the impact on voice. And we describe how to organize apprenticeship in the classroom.

Afterword   159
As an Afterword, we offer our closing thoughts, including some ideas for future work, some ways to bring this work not only into our classrooms but into our lives as readers and writers, and some hopes for students and teachers.

Appendices   171
The appendices include an exploration of usage and an accompanying narrative that demonstrates the conventions described.

Introduction

Teaching Grammar to Achieve Power,
Beauty, and Voice

Grammar is my enemy.

— WILLIAM STAFFORD

We begin with a humbling story:

True to the stages of the writing process, we began this book by collecting. We read articles and books by experts in the field and interviewed teachers, colleagues, and students. We taught in many classrooms, looked at reams of student work, and jotted down pages of notes. We gathered quotes by beloved authors and turned to the books stacked by our beds to uncover examples of writing that manipulated the conventions of grammar to stirring and powerful ends. Friends emailed us poems about punctuation, our families brought us articles they'd read, till we felt like a magnet for all that was new and provocative about grammar and were filled with that exhilarating feeling you get when you're deep in a project, when everything you set your eyes upon seems to speak to you, suggesting connections and possibilities you have never quite noticed before.

And so we were not entirely surprised to find a story online one day about the connection between grammar and success that was based on a study of top Fortune 500 executives' command of grammar. We went to the site and found the report accompanied by a link to an online quiz that would test our own knowledge of usage in order to predict how successful we would be in the world of the workplace. We clicked on the link, confident of our ability to score well on a grammar quiz; we were, after all, highly literate people—teachers of English and lovers of books, with published work to our names, two intelligent women who could wield a semicolon and had a rather rakish way with dashes.

But then the trouble began.

The quiz consisted of a series of sentences, some "correct" and some "incorrect," and we had to choose which were which. Some had mistakes that were easy to spot—a possessive *its* spelled like the contraction *it's*, a *who* instead of a *whom*, an introductory phrase that was missing a comma, a plural verb with a singular subject—but others seemed far trickier. There were sentences that looked right but we sensed were somehow wrong, with errors that we couldn't quite pinpoint, let alone technically define. There were sentences with an abundance of commas, none of which seemed truly wrong, though the sheer number of them suggested that something was, indeed, amiss. And so we made our way through the quiz with a growing sense of foreboding and the kind of queasiness students feel when told to fully underline the predicate in a sentence.

The good news was that we scored rather well. The bad news was that the quiz exposed our own sometimes slippery understanding of and sympathy for proper conventions, revealing our uncertainty more than our expertise and making us each wonder if we needed to run out and find a new copy of Strunk and White. How could we write a book about teaching grammar when our own usage wasn't perfectly consistent?

This quandary only deepened when a new book came our way. The book was called *Eats, Shoots and Leaves*, a "Runaway #1 British Bestseller," according to the book's cover, that was now climbing bestseller charts here. The title was based on a joke about a panda who is forced to pursue an outlaw lifestyle as a result of a misplaced comma in a wildlife guide, and we found that anecdote, like much of the book, hilarious. The author, Lynne Truss (2003), makes a passionate case for the importance of punctuation, while dotting her book with winsome mistakes, like "Dicks in tray" and "Children drive slowly." By her own admission, she is a "stickler," one of those who advocate a zero-tolerance approach to punctuation errors, and her book is an unapologetic call to arms, where she goes so far as to say that fellow sticklers should carry a red pen with them at all times to publicly cross out misplaced apostrophes or add them whenever they're needed.

Again, there was something appealing—and funny—in the thought of a band of punctuation vigilantes safeguarding the world from the kind of confusions that are borne of grammatical mistakes. But there was also something problematic about it, something elitist, like a club closed to all who can't define the difference between a phrase and a clause. And it raised some questions: Were we sticklers? And, red pens notwithstanding, were most teachers? And if we weren't, should we be?

Certainly Lynne Truss thinks so. She blames pedagogues for what she sees as the dangerous decline in proper punctuation usage; we are the reason, she implies, that dicks are lying around in trays. Yet something about this strikes us as unfair, if only because it's too simple. A stickler, for instance, would take issue with the split infinitive two paragraphs back (*to publicly cross out* instead of *to cross out publicly*). But to a generation raised on episodes of *Star Trek*, in which the starship *Enterprise* dares *to boldly go* where no man has gone before, does it matter if we split infinitives—especially when "to boldly go" sounds more bold and intrepid to our ears than "to go boldly" does? Is this really a marker of civilization's end, as Lynne Truss might have it, an erosion of culture akin to fast food and elevator music and the smiley faces made of punctuation marks that litter instant messages? Or is this grammatical injunction antiquated, a rule that no longer holds cultural weight, except to a fussy few, like the fashion injunction to never wear white before Memorial Day nor after the first of September? Or was it never a rule but simply a common taste? Is grammar, finally, all a matter of taste, a personal or communal preference, of the sort that editor John Rosenthal (2004) mentions in a recent op-ed piece in the *Times*, where he notes that two pillars of proper usage, the *New Yorker* and the *New York Times*, hold different positions on serial commas (the ones separating, for instance, *peas, corn,* and *potatoes*), with the *New Yorker* always inserting a comma before the *and* while the *New York Times* omits it?

We grappled with these questions for a long time—and, in fact, are grappling with them still, though we did reach the following conclusion: We believe that the beauty of language in general, and of English in particular, is that it is a living, breathing thing, always ready to expand and evolve and change to accommodate new forms of expression. As teachers, we do our students a disservice not to apprise them of the standards and rules of written English that dominant society endorses—and that they, themselves, might be judged by. But given that our language and our culture are in flux and changing rapidly, we serve students best when we empower them to make purposeful choices and decisions based on a complex, nuanced understanding of the effects those grammatical choices will have on both our minds and our hearts and the way they can affect and reinforce meaning. And so we offer the following thoughts about when and where to embed grammar instruction in reading and writing classrooms, and how to do it in a way that supports our most empowering goals, which include helping students achieve power, beauty, and voice.

Grammar and the Culture of Power

Through our reading, writing, and teaching we have come to understand that grammar is intimately linked with power. Power inhabits the linguistic codes a culture accepts. And control of grammar confers access. Lisa Delpit, in *Other People's Children* (1995), argues that "there are codes or rules for participating in power; that is, there is a 'culture of power' " (24). Delpit pleads for teachers to instruct students, particularly students of color and poor students, in the literacy codes they need in order to have access to upper-level education and jobs. Without this kind of access, these students endure closed doors and are denied opportunities, including the opportunity to alter the status quo. From Delpit, we have learned to acknowledge that there is, indeed, a culture of power and that language is one of its gatekeepers.

We add that there are factors other than language that bar these doors—factors such as color and pedigree and religion and gender and sexual identity. But control of language is something we can teach, and we can teach it, moreover, in such a way that student voices may become powerful, disruptive forces. Delpit writes that

> students must be *taught* the codes needed to participate fully in the mainstream of American life, not by being forced to attend to hollow, inane, decontextualized subskills, but rather within the context of meaningful communicative endeavors: that they must be allowed the resource of the teacher's

expert knowledge, while being helped to acknowledge their own "expertness" as well; and that even while students are assisted in learning the culture of power, they must also be helped to learn about the arbitrariness of those codes and about the power relationships they represent. (45)

Acknowledging a culture of power and its linguistic codes means prefacing grammar instruction with an examination of the ways judgment accompanies usage (proper grammar). We can talk about the rules of grammar as being more than language rules: they are cultural norms. We can show students how style manuals like those by Strunk and White (2000), Amis (1997), and Fowler and Fowler ([1906] 2002) defined *modern usage* as the set of language rules they codified. We can use these books as references to answer questions we may have about usage. But these guides, like all texts, are never neutral or culturally unbiased. We had always, for instance, thought that Strunk and White offered writers sound advice. Try to write with clarity and conciseness, they said; choose plain words over fancy ones. Yet on reading an interview with Harold Bloom in Ben Yagoda's new book, *The Sound on the Page: Style and Voice in Writing*, that advice suddenly sounded suspect. Of Strunk and White, Bloom says:

> If I were asked to sum up its teachings, they would be: put yourself in the background, avoid all figurative language if possible, and don't be opinionated . . . it outlaws everything I care about in the writing, in literature, in the act of writing . . .
>
> If you can get yourself to write like that and admire writing like that, then you must be a gentleman or gentlewoman, rather than a parvenu. I had a creepy feeling as I browsed in it. Those qualities which the latter half is rejecting, and which are my essence as a human being, a writer and a teacher— those are exactly the qualities that Yale would not tolerate in me. That tells me what this is. The genteel tradition—or the Gentile tradition—is what Strunk and White comes down to. (2004, xxi)

Bloom points to the linguistic purity protected by style manuals, a purity that is not neutral, but has its roots in Puritanism, in the King's English and its defenders, and that works to contain and restrain the strange, the new, and the different. And so we are careful, when we talk about "proper" grammar and the language of power with students, to show that there are writers and artists who abandon or subvert modern usage to achieve other purposes. We consider what happens when writers break the rules, and how language and power are continually shifting. We look at the forces that affect these shifts and the assumptions that lie beneath them. We think of how impoverished the world would be if the current spectrum of rich, diverse voices were corralled down to one narrow style. And so we consider the role of art in offering alternatives. We talk about Toni Morrison's notion, as she puts it in *Playing in the Dark: Whiteness and the Literary Imagination*, that "in a wholly racialized society, there is no escape from racially inflected language, and the work writers do to unhobble their imagination from the demands of that language is complicated, interesting, and definitive" (1993, 13). Teaching students the language of power does not necessarily mean asking them to conform to it. It means giving them the knowledge they will need to make informed and meaningful language choices.

We also consider what it means to say that writing is "good." Gloria Ladson-Billings, in *The Dreamkeepers: Successful Teachers of African American Children* (1994), addresses the cultural norms that affect teachers throughout the school day as we decide what is good—good grammar, good writing, good behavior, good students, good homes, good values. She decries the idea that teaching is neutral or that students experience school as a place where all students' knowledge or cultures are valued equally. Ladson-Billings sympathizes with the many teachers who "are uncomfortable acknowledging any student differences and particularly racial differences" (31). But she also shows that with the mistaken idea that education and society are free of privilege, teachers sometimes do little to help students understand the forces of racism and privilege in their lives and on their futures (31). Toni Morrison says this also, asserting that "all of us, readers and writers, are bereft when criticism remains too polite or too fearful" (1993, 91).

What might it mean in our teaching of writing to consider language as inflected with cultural norms and teaching as a political act? Delpit tells a cautionary tale in which a black student shaped a narrative that was judged by some adult assessors to be lively and pleasing in its rich description, its nonlinear shifts, and its free associations. It was judged this way by the members of the assessment team who were black. The white members thought this same narrative, because it was not topic-centered and didn't follow a linear structure, suggested that the child had "language problems" and probably also "family problems" and "emotional problems" (1995, 55).

This tale haunts us in the way it shows that goodness is loaded with cultural meanings and values. And so we find ourselves, in assessing grammar and teaching, reassessing how our own cultural literacy pervades what we praise. We look over the writers of works we suggested initially as mentor texts, and we realize that there, too, we see privilege and remnants of a canon that merits further dismantling. We reconsider a chapter heading, a phrase from Strunk and White that admonishes writers to "take pains to admire what is good" (2000, 70). But now we see that the kind of "good" advocated by Strunk and White would condemn the unique beauty we see in the language of Sandra Cisneros—the long, lingering sentences that sometimes do run on, the wordplay, the ambiguous meanings that reside in her phrases. And this "good" would reject Nikki Grimes's skipping language, with its dissonance and its sharpness, as well as Ramona Sapphire's raw, gritty prose, which, despite its surface nihilism and harshness, leads to transcendence and hope. It would also question the stylistic judgment of canonical authors such as Faulkner and Joyce who use elaboration, obfuscation, and even obscurity to powerful literary ends. Thus, in upholding clarity as the greatest virtue, we would miss many other alternative beauties, and reading and writing would be the poorer for this loss.

Meaning and Voice

These are intense tasks to sustain in our work as teachers—to examine and teach language as a cultural code and to try to do it in such a way that we maintain the potential for both appreciating and interrupting the very codes we study. We find that we can teach grammar organically this way if our literacy work is informed by certain critical reading and liberating writing practices (Currie 1998; Scholes 1989; Sedgwick 1990). And so, in reading, we consider things like the importance of metaphor—not in the small technical sense of the term, as a figure of speech that compares two things, but in its broader applications: metaphor as a way of finding meaning in the world, of seeing how stories refer to experiences larger than their own particulars—and try to understand why images linger in our hearts long after we close a book because they speak to more than just what was on the page. We read thinking about social norms and their power in the text and in our lives, such as how we learn about social status and the rules that accompany gender, and what meanings are attached to color. We read thinking about identities, and which identities come to flourish in school, in our neighborhoods, in our families and lives, and why. And we read asking about power—who has it, how it is held, how it shifts. Thus we look for subtexts as we read texts, and the possible meanings that reside in them, considering, all the while, what we bring to the text and how we come away changed.

In teaching writing, we teach that students' lives are worth writing about and that writing is one way to observe current conditions and imagine others. We teach the role of story in fostering empathy, and we consider ways to develop sympathetic imaginations as writers (Greene 1995; Ehrenworth 2003). We teach students diverse genres and various craft techniques. We teach that we write our stories in order to know ourselves better, and that we write for others to imagine experiences with which they are unfamiliar. We teach that writing is one way to express outrage and to bear witness, and that writing is a way to find moments of beauty and hold onto them. We teach that we can study writing as a subject and by doing so, we can make our voices more powerful.

And so we embed our grammar instruction in reading and writing practices that help students develop lucid and powerful voices. But what, precisely, do we mean by "voice"? How do we define it? Frequently teachers say simply that we know it when we see it, and this statement carries some truth. In the aftermath of September 11, for instance, the New York City public schools were flooded with letters of support from children around the world. The letters came in all sizes and envelopes, some addressed with nothing more scribbled on them than "To a School by the Twin Towers, New York, New York." It was a consolation, in those days of fear and grief, to sit at a table at a district office with colleagues and read those outpourings of sympathy. As literacy educators working in the upper grades, however, we found ourselves struck by something that had more to do with voice than content. We noted that the most moving letters came from younger children, like Tyler, age 6, from Augusta, Maine:

> I got these two bunnies for Easter. I gave them love and snuggles and they made me feel safe. Now I give them to you so you're happy. I hope they help you feel safe, too. (Harwayne 2002, x)

Tyler's writing reaches out to strangers, across miles and borders, to offer words of commiseration in the belief that it is, indeed, possible for one human being to help another. Many young writers in these letters shared their fears and hopes with us and offered their own methods for coping, all in the most heartfelt and personal of ways. We felt their presence on the page. Their writing instilled belief in the possibility of goodness. Yet the letters that came from older students seemed more perfunctory and anonymous. They relied on standard words of condolence and frequently referred to other moments in history, most notably the Civil War, as if such citations could act as proof that they understood the enormity of what had happened. We did not doubt their good intentions, nor question the depth of their feelings—they had, after all, been moved enough to take the time to write to someone that they didn't even know, yet their words conveyed none of that. There was little voice and little emotion, little life that came off the page, and we found ourselves pondering the implications. If younger children were more unabashed than adolescents as writers, why? Why were their voices more powerful? How did they, as writers, find the courage and hope to believe, or offer the belief, that a stuffed bunny could really assuage a city's grief? Adolescence is a complicated nexus of anxiety and self-consciousness. We remember that; we see it in our students and in our own children. But looking at student writing, we also see the tracks of teaching, and as we sat at this table, in the face of overwhelming evidence that the longer students had been in school, the less their writing moved us, we had to ask: As these students got older, was there something inherent in schooling itself that stripped them of their voices? Were too many classrooms sacrificing risk taking and original thought for conformity?

In our current climate of standardized tests, merit pay, and stricter rules about promotion, we understand that the stakes are high and that the pressure to have students "succeed" in academic ways is enormous. Yet here is a curious fact: While studying state standardized language arts tests nationwide, we found that in almost every state, students can achieve the higher scores in writing (be it for a persuasive essay, a letter, a literary essay, or a narrative) only if their writing demonstrates that elusive quality known as voice. In rubric after rubric, the upper scores are reserved for those writers whose language is lively and engaging, whose sentences are varied, and whose overall structure demonstrates not only clarity but a dynamic sense of purpose. None of these qualities is described in the directions for the writing tasks, where students are given a prompt and often a set of bullets that offers a conventional structure. They are usually told in the directions to write a well-organized piece that fully answers the prompt and that uses examples as directed. Nowhere are they directed to write with voice. Nowhere are they told that writers with voice—writers with flair and imagination and style—will be more successful than those who write with just competence. And denying that explicit information to students—and to teachers, as well—helps maintain a status quo that leaves less knowledgeable students at a distinct disadvantage.

Resistance and Recuperation

So we commit ourselves to teaching voice, which, beyond its more ineffable traits having to do with personality, is composed of word choice, punctuation, and syntax—in other words, partly of grammar. We consider, thus, how grammar matters not only for how it transfers power but for its intrinsic beauty and its revelatory qualities. But how do we convey this to students? One immediate way is to recover grammar from its current position, where it languishes in dog-eared workbooks and editing handouts and checklists. Editing is the act of applying knowledge of conventions to writing that is near publication. But if, as we believe, grammar is linked to voice, students need to be thinking about grammar far earlier in the writing process. We cannot teach grammar in lasting ways if we teach it as a way to *fix* student writing, especially writing they view as already complete. Students need to construct knowledge of grammar by practicing it as part of what it means to write, particularly in how it helps create a voice that engages a reader on the page.

Too often, though, in our early research, we heard a note of despair whenever teachers talked about grammar, a feeling of frustration that came through in remarks such as "These kids just don't care," and "Didn't anybody ever teach these kids anything?" We have to say instead, that if we are teaching grammar, and the students are not learning grammar from us, then there is something wrong with the way we are teaching it. Our research, therefore, was founded on a belief in children's ability to learn. We assumed either that there was something confusing or insubstantial in our teaching or that students understood grammar but did not like it. Delpit tells of some fourth graders she studied, who, as she described it, "had the *competence* to express themselves in a more standard form, but chose, consciously or unconsciously, to use the language of those in their local environments" (1995, 52).

We saw some of this—that the influence of peer cultures, in particular, was at odds with an academic culture, and that students chose to fit in with their peers or relations by adopting locally accepted language codes. Their language choices, we saw, were often indicative of performance rather than competence. These kids were smart. They learned many things. They knew many things, and they were making complicated, finely nuanced judgments. Pedro Noguera, in *City Schools and the American Dream: Reclaiming the Promise of Public Education* (2003), affirms this as a common and invisible struggle, in which students resist language, habits, or learning practices that they fear will be deemed assimilationist.

But we also saw something else, a smaller power skirmish. We saw that many students experienced grammar instruction as teachers holding up a piece of student writing and modeling how to "fix" it. Our lessons were not really instruction so much as correction. We offered grammar as a set of rules that demands acquiescence. There was some acquiescence, but there was more resistance. There is resistance in Delpit's fourth graders who reject standard English. There is resistance in Jenny, who completes the workbook assignment on subject-verb agreement accurately but makes no attempt to sustain subject-verb agreement in her own writing. There is resistance in Efram, who writes rap songs that are long, and carefully crafted, and subject to revision, but refuses to do this same work with writing for school.

There is resistance in all of these acts, and there is possibility. Heshusius, a researcher in resistance theory, describes a paradigm for reconceptualizing incompetence, inability, and sometimes misbehavior. She writes:

> Resistance theory provides a framework for understanding these children's behavior as active resistance to a situation they find threatening, boring, or otherwise intolerable. (1989, 409)

It is possible, for instance, to view the ways that students resist oppressive learning experiences as imaginative and as significant. Maxine Greene, in "Imagining Futures: The Public School and Possibility," says, "When we think of the boredom in US high schools and the nihilism that can and has led to fearsome violence, we need to explore the ways there are of overcoming senseless fury at existing conditions, feelings of pointlessness, even despair" (2000, 273). It is hopeless to impose curriculum on adolescents. We need to invite them, tempt them, and seduce them. Pedro Noguera and Maxine Greene talk about what an act of faith it is that some teenagers come to school at all. We need to do everything possible to make school a place where they experience at least some moments of surprise, beauty, and joy, and where they learn things that empower them in their diverse and extraordinary lives.

It is possible to invite students into the recuperation of grammar. We may invite them by demonstrating how knowledge of grammar grants access to power. We may tempt them by showing how grammar is an art or excite them by demonstrating how, to us, teaching is a love affair with words. And we may seduce them with story.

The Sway of Story

Stories, the telling and the writing of them, are how students attach meaning to our lessons; they are where students see the impact of grammatical choices and where we ensconce this work in the luminous. The sway of stories is tremendous. In *The Child That Books Built*, Francis Spufford says, "We tell stories all the time when we speak. Storytelling may be the function that made language worth acquiring" (2002, 46). Spufford goes on to describe the impact of stories on his adolescence: "The books you read as a child brought you sights you hadn't seen yourself, scents you hadn't smelled, sounds you hadn't heard. They introduced you to people you hadn't met, and helped you to sample ways of being that would never have occurred to you" (10). Not only do we imagine lives other than our own through stories, but stories help us value those lives. It is in the act of disentangling the meanings that reside in the stories we read, and limning meaning in the stories we write, that we demonstrate that it is worth contending with language.

We have come to realize that the choices we make as to what stories we read and tell in the classroom are ethical choices. Audrey Thompson writes that "stories have enormous moral power. Sometimes the power lies in the resonance and familiarity of a story, its capacity to describe what we know or believe; sometimes the power of a story lies in its rich complexity and its capacity to show us things we never saw before" (1998, 537). We try to read and write stories that widen the choices that seem possible to adolescents as they construct their identities. We try to read and write stories that illuminate struggle, that acknowledge difference and the meanings that come to be attached to difference. We admit what bell hooks contends in *Teaching to Transgress* (1994): that school, like the world, is never safe for everyone at the same time. It is from deep within this unsafe place that we realize the significance of one of our most fundamental beliefs: writers take risks.

The stories we tell and write integrate the urgent social issues that shape the lives of adolescents. Some of these stories tell of moments of confusion, desire, or danger. Some reveal glimpses of beauty. Some disclose moments of loss or the foretaste of sudden, new understanding. We write from the hearts of the children we were and the students we see every day. We cull our past, we consider the stories we have read, heard, and observed, looking for those that feel familiar. We recall, we dream, we fictionalize, we do the work writers do as they struggle to concoct a story that others want to hear. In some ways, this is the most important part of our work, for it is in the encounter with story that all the rest falls into place. It is in the heart of a story that students accompany us as we struggle with form and with meaning and they see the paths that lie before them in their own work.

And because curriculum is a complicated and multilayered thing, it is also in story that students envision possibilities aside from, or intimately conjoined with, the force of language. For adolescents learn about identity, they learn about choice, they learn about possibility and impossibility through the stories they encounter in school. We know this. We know it from the stories we have inhabited and the ones we cannot find. And so we try to tell our stories bravely, so that the placement of a comma matters, so that an apostrophe marks the possession of the heart as well as the mind.

A Framework for Readers

As you move forward in the text, you will face the need to consider how you wish to incorporate and implement the work described in the following chapters. While we share plans and lessons, our goal is not to hold up those plans and lessons as final, but to encourage the individual exploration and teaching of grammar. We have come to some conclusions in our research, and it is always both a relief and a danger to have come to conclusions. We offer certain methodologies as ones we have found effective. We share certain ways to design lessons that we have learned from others. We share texts that we have found to be generative in the classroom. But we do this with some apprehension that these will be taken as definitive. We intend them as invitational and provisional. Instruction, like writing, is organic. It is also a love affair. It is a love affair with books, with adolescents, with language, with our lives, their lives, and the world.

Putting Conventions in Our In-Tray

Planning Grammar Curriculum

2

> The defense of language is too large a matter to be left to the properly qualified.
>
> — KINGSLEY AMIS

These are our goals for teaching grammar: to teach knowledge of conventional usage in order to increase power, opportunity, and voice; to teach habits of fluency, inquiry, and experimentation; and to engage students in such a way that this knowledge and these habits are sustaining and flexible. We plan for this kind of heady work, if only to ensure that we make space in the curriculum for it. We may be anxious. We may feel that our own grasp of grammar is too tenuous to really impart knowledge in empowering ways. We may worry that we will be too tentative or that we will be too didactic. We may worry that we will be boring. But we need to do it. We cannot deny student writers knowledge of practices that inform our own writing. If our execution falls short of our plans at times, if there is struggle, that simply means we are striving, and that is a good thing.

And so we come to planning. There is an art to planning. Dewey says, "A large part of the art of instruction lies in making the difficulty of new problems large enough to challenge thought, and small enough so that, in addition to the confusion naturally attending the novel elements, there shall be luminous familiar spots from which helpful suggestions may spring" ([1916] 1944, 157). Careful plans are strategic. Strategic plans link new curriculum to ongoing studies and familiar practices, so that students can fit new understandings into the long-term development of fluency. Yet strategic plans also introduce some studies as unfamiliar or radical, so that students experience the classroom and language as provocative. We want to demonstrate that learning is the process of continually remaining open to new ways of looking.

And so we offer several ways to plan grammar instruction. The familiar spot from which we launch this work is writing workshop. We imagine all of the following lessons as embedded within beliefs and practices that empower student writers to achieve meaning, beauty, and knowledge through writing. Our plans for grammatical instruction, therefore, coincide with our curriculum calendar for writing workshop.

By a curriculum calendar for writing workshop, we mean that we teach writing as a subject, and we plan the year as several units of study, with each unit of study representing at least one opportunity for students to publish, as well as an opportunity to study genres, authors, or craft deeply. There are many useful guides to planning units of study in writing workshop, including Nancie Atwell's *In the Middle* (1998), Lucy Calkins's *The Art of Teaching Writing* (1996), Katie Wood Ray's *What You Know by Heart* (2002), and Heather Lattimer's *Thinking Through Genre* (2003). We have often mapped a yearlong writing curriculum so that it looks like the table on page 17.

In general, we break up the year with units of study so that students write to publish and so that students learn a variety of purposes, structures, and craft techniques as writers. Within each unit of study, we plan to teach some writing lessons on finding meaningful subjects; making genre decisions and considering structure; crafting and revising; and getting ready to publish. We teach these lessons as students are moving at diverse paces through stages of collecting; drafting; revising; and working on presentation.

We particularly like the descriptions of writing process and its implications for teaching offered by Don Murray in *A Writer Teaches Writing* (1985). Murray writes:

> Writing is not superficial to the intellectual life but central to it; writing is one of the most disciplined ways of making meaning and one of the most effective methods we can use to monitor our own thinking.
>
> We write to think—to be surprised by what appears on the page; to explore our world with language; to discover meaning that teaches us and that

UNIT 1	(September–October):	*Memoir and narrative structures*
UNIT 2	(October–November):	*Essay and nonnarrative structures*
UNIT 3	(December):	*Writing about literature*
UNIT 4	(January–February):	*Short fiction*
UNIT 5	(March):	*Journalism*
UNIT 6	(April):	*Poetry*
UNIT 7	(May–June):	*Open genre or multigenre projects*

may be worth sharing with others. We do *not* know what we want to say before we say it; we write to know what we want to say. (3)

It is within this theory of teaching writing that we consider grammar instruction, and so we believe that learning grammar must be linked to the process of discovery, to intellectual thought. As a series of received ideas, grammar instruction has little impact—students must construct knowledge of grammar as they discover what it means to write. Murray adds:

> Writing is a craft before it is an art; writing may appear magic, but it is our responsibility to take our students backstage to watch the pigeons being tucked up the magician's sleeve. The process of writing can be studied and understood. We can recreate most of what a student or professional writer does to produce effective writing.
>
> The process is not linear, but recursive. The writer passes through the process once, or many times, emphasizing different stages during each passage. (4)

And so we turn also to Murray for the notion that we can teach writing and its processes as a subject and that writing consists of different stages that the writer circles through. In the plans that follow we lift grammar instruction out of the editing phase and move it into earlier stages of the writing process. Teaching editing, we believe, means teaching students to review their writing using their knowledge of conventions. But they need to learn these conventions earlier in the writing process as strategies for making clarity and meaning. And, ideally, both they and we need to see how grammar can be not just a corrective tool but an inspiring, transformative one.

Teaching Toward Fluency

Planning grammar instruction, or any instruction, leads to consideration of methodology, as in *how* we will teach. We find it useful to think of our work as fitting into three categories: *direct instruction; inquiry;* and *apprenticeship*. By *direct instruction*, we mean lessons in which we tell students explicitly how to do something, based on our knowledge of language and how writers control it. So, for instance, we may explain and demonstrate that writers need consistent verb endings to maintain verb tense. *Inquiry* means lessons in which we facilitate investigations of language. An investigation into how some writers manipulate verb tense to create specific effects is an inquiry. *Apprenticeship* means teaching students to mentor themselves to published writers, to adapt their style as a way to explore form and voice. These categories are loose ones; individual lessons may cross these boundaries.

Much of our planning supports direct instruction, perhaps because this method feels the most efficient. Lisa Delpit describes the acquisition of linguistic powers thus: "Unless one has the leisure of a lifetime of 'immersion' to learn them, explicit presentation makes learning immeasurably easier." She goes on to say that, "in literacy instruction, explicitness might be equated with direct instruction" (1995, 26–27). When we plan direct instruction we plan in response to assessment and to our knowledge of conventions. For instance, let us imagine that we are launching writing workshop at the beginning of the year with a new class of students. Let us imagine that their demonstration of conventions is diverse and creative—what some might call faulty—and often this makes it hard to understand their writing. Once most of our students are committed to saying something they find meaningful in their writing, we want to teach them ways to write more effectively. The time and energy needed to get our students to the comma in the previous sentence, of course, may be intense. But if our students aren't invested in their subjects, it is unlikely they will invest in grammar. That is why our first writing unit will be full of many other lessons aimed at helping students discover their subjects, and the grammar lessons will come later, during revision.

To be clear, we are not separating out conventions from the writing process. Achieving power over conventions is essential to writing meaningfully, and these lessons merit attention within the writing process. And so we teach within writing workshop, offering minilessons on how writers control conventions. For instance, with direct instruction we can teach students to make meaningful choices about ending punctuation as a revision lesson. Then in our second unit, we teach students that writers don't wait for revision to make these choices about ending punctuation; we do this work while drafting. Then in our third writing unit, we show students how fluent writers make these choices even as we write for the first time. Thus we plan for, demonstrate, and coach the habits of fluency.

We can apply this kind of planning to any direct instruction in strategies writers use to make their writing more effective, including not just punctuation but also parts of a sentence, the use of paragraphs and other internal structures, and spelling. Thus, if we plan to teach some spelling strategies in our first unit during revision, we move in the next unit to teaching students to use these same strategies while drafting, then in our third unit we encourage students to use these spelling strategies as they freewrite and always as they write. This kind of planning gives us a way to deeply and strategically embed the many thoughtful lessons offered in texts such as Diane Snowball and Faye Bolton's *Spelling K–8* (1999), Janet Angelillo's *A Fresh Approach to Teaching Punctuation* (2002), and Constance Weaver's *Teaching Grammar in Context* (1996).

So we have now a method for long-term planning that is surprisingly easy and lets us build into our curriculum immediately any instruction that profitably starts as revision work. We follow Don Murray's (1997) and Georgia Heard's (2002) idea that revision is a way of reseeing in order to discover and create meaning. Revision is the opportunity to restructure, reword, play, plan, and imagine it differently. It is a fruitful time in the writing process to consider the impact of grammatical decisions and the opportunities they imply, which brings us to the lesson plan.

Before we look at an actual direct instruction lesson more closely, though, and how it changes as we move it up in the writing process, we want to insert two small cautions: First, some teaching of grammar shouldn't begin as revision work; it should begin someplace else in the writing process and the curriculum. Grammar is a large and beautiful subject. Sometimes it is about aesthetics, and the aesthetic is rarely served well by direct instruction. And so we will look at this kind of work separately when we consider inquiry and apprenticeship. Our second caution is this: we need to show students other meaningful ways to revise their writing, ways that fit the genres they have chosen and the meanings they are striving for. Our favorite texts for teaching powerful, and liberating, revision strategies are Don Murray's *The Craft of Revision* (1997) and Georgia Heard's *The Revision Toolbox* (2002). Later in this book we look at the unexpected ways writers achieve voice and meaning through grammar—these strategies would qualify as artful revision. Here, though, we are starting with the comprehensibility and power achieved through controlling conventions, what Lisa Delpit calls "useful and usable knowledge which contributes to a student's ability to communicate effectively in standard, generally acceptable literary forms" (1995, 19).

Writers Making Effective Choices: Establishing Tone

As we launch writing workshop, a critical lesson for students of any age is one on beginning and ending sentences by using a capital to mark the beginning and ending punctuation (period, question mark, or exclamation point) at the end. This is a lesson we can insert when we get to revision in our first unit. Some readers may think, "I would never teach that lesson in secondary school—students should have had that lesson in second grade!" This may be true. Yet we ask you to look at your students' writing at the beginning of the year and assess if they are all, in fact, using ending punctuation in appropriate, consistent, and effective ways. If they are, start with one of the more advanced lessons on usage that we present in the following chapter. Our own experience is that rarely are middle and high school students consistently using ending punctuation well. In many classrooms, we see ending punctuation that is erratic. And in most classrooms, including those with highly fluent writers, we see students who would be more powerful writers if they made more careful and informed choices.

What we do, therefore, is teach a lesson on ending punctuation that benefits both more and less fluent writers. We teach ending punctuation in such a way that it introduces its usage to writers who have not mastered it, and we demonstrate the various stylistic effects of ending punctuation at the same time, so that fluent writers benefit from the lesson as well. This matters: we try to never introduce a lesson as a punitive, language-police kind of lesson where we hold up the students' writing to show how it needs to be fixed. That sets up resistance. We don't need to hold up flawed student writing to validate the idea that writers make punctuation choices. It is also a hopeless fantasy to imagine that students aren't doing something simply because no one has told them how. More commonly, students have been taught capitalization and ending punctuation, but they are not retaining the information or demonstrating mastery. Therefore, the structure of our lesson and the tone of our approach matter. We may yearn to just tell them again to use capitals and periods, dammit! We may consider the I'm-sure-you-just-overlooked-this-it's-so-obvious tone. Or the you-were-probably-just-rushing-because-you-have-so-much-to-say tone. Or the outraged didn't-anyone-last-year-teach-you-anything tone. Or, worse, the where-did-you-come-from-that-you-don't-know-this tone. Unfortunately, these are common tones in grammar instruction.

A less frequently heard tone is one in which we are serious and we value students' perceptions and their need to learn. We try to always ground our grammar lessons in the notion that *writers make choices*. Thus, a lesson that was in danger of becoming "You need to use capitals and periods, because no one can understand your writing" becomes instead "In expanding our powers as writers, we make significant choices even at the sentence level." Our goal is a tone that is constructive, affirmative, urgent. Just shifting from *you* to *we* in that way constructs a community of writers. Then we also link conventions to power and the ability to make effective choices. Tone matters.

We consider and discuss tone in all our teaching of reading and writing in order to model for our students how tone affects us. The tone we set in classrooms is critical for our students' welfare and engagement. And tone is critical in all writing. We respond to it, just as we respond to a teacher's kind or harsh word. And like the tone that we set in classrooms, a writer's tone is built around word choice, as well as punctuation, sentence structure, and syntax—around *how* we convey *what* it is we want to say to add more grace and meaning.

In the lessons that follow we spend much time talking with students about tone and voice, considering how changes in punctuation and grammar will affect them in meaningful ways. We are aware, however, that talking about tone is not always commonplace in classrooms, and teachers and students alike may feel a bit discomfited at first. We believe, though, that as readers we are always responding to tone, even if it's at a gut level. We warm to tones we find inviting and abandon books whose tone we find cold. We react to things like sentence length and paragraphing each in our own unique way, some of us loving long, meandering sentences while others find them ponderous. And so we show our students how, as readers, we make sense of all kinds of texts, by sharing the inner workings of our minds and pinning language to our previously unspoken thoughts. And then we articulate for our students how we engage as writers with texts of our own making.

The good news is that there's really not a wrong way to do this, provided that we honestly attempt to say what we feel and think. It is not even wrong to confess to students that this is something new we're trying, something we're experimenting with, because we know that writers do it, too. To make this work a bit easier to take on, we have written the following lessons out in full, with the actual words we would say, as a way of modeling precisely and clearly just how such lessons might sound.

Lesson Design and Storytelling

Here is one way a direct instruction grammar lesson might sound and look. It follows a minilesson design developed at the Teachers College Reading and Writing Project (Calkins and Teachers College 2003) in the way it *connects* the lesson to the students' prior work, then makes a *teaching point* that includes a demonstration, then gives students an opportunity to process the lesson through some *active involvement,* and then *links* the lesson to their ongoing work as writers. There are many ways to design lessons. We offer this plan as one possibility, one that helps us envision the sticky parts and think about the language we will choose and the examples we will use.

What is invisible in this plan, though, is the attention we have paid to what stories we tell in our demonstrations. These stories are strategic. We model our lessons with stories that are worth revisiting. We model with stories that engage adolescents because they are stories of childhood, stories about power, about identity, about desire and danger and beauty. The lesson design is how we map out what we will say when. The story we tell is the heart of our teaching. It is where we show that this work is worth doing and that writers take risks. It is how we tempt and seduce and gather our students into the work and into our hearts. In this sample lesson, we return to only one line of our story, but it is the knowledge of the story, the common narrative and the experience it describes, that makes the lesson meaningful. And so a lesson might look like this:

A First Lesson on Ending Punctuation
Writers Make Significant Choices
About Ending Punctuation

Connection and Invitation

So we've been talking a lot about how writers make choices, including how we select our subjects and how we may choose to make certain aspects of our subjects more explicit as we write. You are writing now in such important ways. Some of you are writing about issues of great significance to us all. We'll understand ourselves and others better when we read your writing. And some of you are doing something a bit different, which is that you are writing in such a way that your piece will have the most meaning to you. You are showing us that writing helps us learn about ourselves, and that in learning to tell our own stories well, we clarify things in our own lives.

Now that you have made powerful choices about what you are writing about, and how you are going to say what you want to say, today I want to teach you that writers make significant choices even at the sentence level about what they want their writing to sound like.

Teaching Point and Demonstration

We know that writers capitalize the first word of a new sentence so their readers can clearly recognize that a new sentence is beginning. For the end of the sentence, though, writers have more choice, and the choices they make will affect the tone of their writing. Writers decide whether to use a period, a question mark, or an exclamation point. Watch me look at my own writing and decide which ending punctuation would be better for my piece. Try to watch in such a way that you can describe what I'm doing as a writer. [For older students we may say: You may want to be ready to jot some notes when I'm done. Put them in your writer's notebook under a heading that says "Choosing Ending Punctuation for Sentences."]

As you know, I'm writing this piece about the time in sixth grade when I tore off an alligator from an Izod shirt in an expensive store and sewed it on the shirt I had from Sears so I could sit with the popular kids in the cafeteria at school. Here's the sentence I wrote yesterday:

As I sat in the dressing room, holding the seam ripper, I wondered what would happen if I were caught.

OK, I've capitalized the first letter, that's good—although my handwriting is sort of messy, so I'm going to make it more clear that it's a capital. Now I'm thinking about the ending of the sentence. I can leave it like this, with a period, then it sounds like this: [read aloud as is, matter-of-factly]. OK, I guess if I want to keep the tone kind of matter-of-fact, not too dramatic, I should use a period.

Let's try it with a question mark now. I'll have to change it a bit if I want it to be a question. [Demonstrate, writing the new sentence while speaking.]

> I sat in the dressing room, holding the seam ripper. What would happen if I were caught?

This does make it sound more like I'm questioning the whole situation. It introduces a note of fear, almost. Maybe I want that? Let me see one more. Can I do this with an exclamation point?

> I sat in the dressing room, holding the seam ripper. What would happen if I were caught!

Or

> I sat in the dressing room, holding the seam ripper! What would happen if I were caught!

That exclamation point does make it sound more exciting. Let me think. But maybe that's too exciting for this piece. I'm not trying to write some crime novel here, I'm just trying to tell a rather difficult personal story and think about what it might mean.

Active Engagement and Reflection

Talk to a partner about which punctuation choice you think would be most effective for this sentence and why. Then let's share some ideas (and possibly notes) for how we make effective punctuation choices.

Or

I'm going to move to a different sentence in my piece. With a partner, try it with various ending punctuation, and talk about which one sounds best to you and why. Then we'll make some notes together about the effects of different punctuation.

Or

Talk to your partner a moment about what I just did as a writer—what steps did I follow in trying to choose ending punctuation? How will you make these decisions?

Or

Jot some notes about what I just did, then talk to your partner a moment about what you wrote down as possible steps for choosing effective ending punctuation.

As we move to planning a second grammar lesson for our first unit, we have some common structures that help us plan: the lessons are grounded in the idea that writers make choices; the lessons build on students' strengths as writers; and we demonstrate on stories that become part of the classroom lore. Thus if we do a second grammar lesson in our first unit, we will demonstrate using the same story, and we will follow the same structure for our lesson plan. It will look something like this:

Teaching Point

Writers know that it is easier for readers to read writing that is in chunks. That's why you'll often see writing that has been broken into sections. One way writers make these small sections for the reader is with paragraphs. A paragraph is marked by the first word of the sentence being indented about five spaces to the right. When we want to make a new paragraph, we indent again.

There is no rule about when to paragraph, but writers often decide to start a new paragraph when one of the following happens in their piece. You should probably jot them down. Let's start a list on a new page of our writing notebooks that has a heading "Possible Places to Insert Paragraphs."

when a new character is introduced
when the setting changes
when the time changes
when a new event occurs
when some new idea is introduced
when we want the reader to notice some new information

Let's look at a piece together and consider where we might decide to start a new paragraph or two if we were the writer and we had decided to be considerate of our reader and break our writing into smaller chunks for the reader. Watch me start . . .

You know I've been working on this anecdote about the alligator shirt. Here's how far I've gotten now. I'll put it up on the overhead so you can look at it too. It says . . .

I remember when I was in sixth grade, it was so important to have an alligator shirt—the real thing, an Izod, with a little alligator on the left breast, and you could only get them at one store in our town, this store called Papagallo that was much more expensive than JC Penney and much much more expensive than Sears or Kmart, and the shirts were $65 which was a lot for a short sleeve cotton shirt in 1977. I'm sure there were kids in my school who didn't wear alligator shirts, and maybe didn't even care about alligator shirts, but I didn't know any, and in the group of kids who I thought of as friends, it seemed very important to have one, at least. Lisa and Christina each had about a dozen, and they were the most popular girls in school. My mom brought a shirt home for me one night from Sears, but it had an elephant on the pocket, and she couldn't understand why I burst into tears, tears of sorrow that we didn't have more money and tears of shame that it mattered to me. I didn't wear the shirt with the elephant, but I heard Christina making fun in the cafeteria of kids who had fake shirts, and how if you couldn't have the real thing, you shouldn't try to pretend to be rich. All the kids at the table agreed those shirts were "gay." That weekend, in Papagallo, in the little cubicle dressing room, I tried on one of those Izod shirts which we couldn't afford, there was no way we had the money for it, and I ripped off the alligator and the label and put them in my pocket. Then I took them home and sewed them on the shirt my mom had given me and I sat next to Lisa at lunch the next day.

OK, I'm thinking that this is a rather big piece. I'm happy it's so big because it was hard to write, to tell the truth. I still get flushed thinking about sitting in that dressing room with my mother's seam ripper, which I had also taken. So I'm thrilled to have so much writing on the page. Now I'm going to think about my reader. I want my reader to read slowly and notice everything I'm saying. So let's see where I could paragraph. Let me check that list we made. OK, I guess I could insert a paragraph right before I tell about when my mom brings home a shirt from Sears—she's kind of a new character in my story, and it's something new that happens.

Engagement and Reflection

What do you think? Talk to your partner about where you think another paragraph or a different one could make sense in this piece of writing.
Or
Talk to your partner about some steps I took as I thought about this big piece of writing and the implications of it being so big.

Link to Ongoing Work and Writing Practices

So, we can keep working on appropriate or artful strategies for inserting paragraphs. Perhaps you'll notice how and when other writers make choices about this. Or perhaps you'll do something in your writing that we should all add to our list. But always, if you find yourself writing in big pieces, you have the power to insert some paragraphs.

It's a different teaching point here than in the previous lesson in ending punctuation, but the structure and intent of the lesson are the same—to empower students with the knowledge they need to control conventions and make meaningful choices.

We reteach these lessons throughout the units of study by moving the place of each lesson forward in the writing process. If we teach the lesson on choosing ending punctuation in our first writing unit as a revision lesson, then we reteach it in the second writing unit as a drafting lesson. So it becomes: "Today I want to teach you that writers don't wait for revision to consider how they will begin and end their sentences. Writers use capital letters to start their sentences when they are drafting, and they make significant choices about ending punctuation as they are drafting, too." We embed our lesson, again, in a story. We usually have one story that we work with over an entire writing unit, and sometimes we even return to a story in another unit, taking up the story in a different genre. And so our return to this lesson returns to the same story of the alligator shirt, told first in unit 1, but here we tuck this anecdote into an essay on oppressive peer cultures. This lesson is included at the end of the chapter (see page 43). In our third writing unit we teach this ending punctuation lesson yet again, but now it is a lesson given while the students are still freewriting, and it sounds something like this: "So writers don't wait until they draft to punctuate their sentences. Writers make choices as they freewrite, as a way to develop their writing fluency and to make it a habit of mind to always write clearly and purposefully." And we tell another story, one that pulls our students right into the work. We tell a story about reading, because our unit is on literary essays, but also talk about how our reading has made us remember a story about tackle tag and the learning of desire. This lesson is also included at the chapter end (see page 47).

As with the lesson in ending punctuation, the lesson in paragraphing can be retaught and extended across our writing curriculum. In unit 2 it becomes: "So writers don't wait for revision to choose when to paragraph. We chunk our writing into effective smaller parts as we draft." And in unit 3 this lesson becomes: "So fluent writers begin to habitually write in paragraphs, even as we freewrite. As we develop particular strategies for choosing when to paragraph, we begin to envision how our writing can be chunked, and we make choices as we write."

This progression marks a shift from punctuation as something we consider when we revise, to something we work on as we write, to one of our *habits of mind* as fluent writers. Thus we accomplish a lot by simply planning some direct instruction in punctuation and grammar. We "backward plan," as it were, introducing our teaching as the students gain confidence in their writing, and linking our teaching to their enhanced power as writers. We reteach at each stage of the writing process, varying our lessons a little to relate them to that particular stage of writing. Thus we may foster many habits of mind simply through planned, direct instruction across the year.

From Lessons to Curriculum

If we plan to teach grammar this way, it is often helpful to make a curriculum calendar in which we lay out the lessons we are planning to introduce, reteach, and extend in our writing units. Each lesson appears three times in our curriculum. In the first writing unit, we introduce grammar as two revision lessons. In the second unit, those same lessons reoccur as drafting lessons, and we introduce two new grammar elements in revision. Thus, by the third unit we have lessons during freewriting, drafting, and revision. The calendar on page 30 shows the lessons on usage that we introduce in each unit, which we review in the next chapter. For a more detailed calendar showing when we reteach each lesson, see pages 44–45.

We're saving unit 7 for teaching artful grammar and ways to break the rules, so we don't include new direct instruction there, we only return to lessons already introduced. Once we have this overall plan for our direct instruction, then we can map each lesson as a revision lesson when it is introduced, as a drafting lesson in the next unit, and as a lesson on fluency in the next. So we can plan accordingly to fit these lessons into the other, non-grammar-related lessons we plan for our writing units. We're ensuring that we plan to teach and reinforce grammar. A sample of this kind of plan is placed at the end of this chapter (pages 44–45).

Another advantage of doing this kind of calendar is that we begin to envision the work that qualifies as inquiry work. For instance, while we can do direct instruction on what fragments are, the students would benefit from inquiry work on when fragments are appropriate and how writers use them. The same could be said of how and why writers use commas. It is one thing to simply instruct on the proper use of commas in sentences containing lists and clauses. It is an entirely different task to convey the artistic way that commas are manipulated to achieve mood, meaning, and voice.

UNIT 1:	*Memoir*
	ending punctuation
	paragraphing

UNIT 2:	*Essay*
	parts of speech
	subject and predicate
	fragments

UNIT 3:	*Writing About Literature*
	subject-verb agreement
	subject and object
	pronoun forms

UNIT 4:	*Short Fiction*
	verb tenses and forms
	punctuating dialogue

UNIT 5:	*Journalism*
	commas in lists
	commas and conjunctions

UNIT 6:	*Poetry*
	apostrophes
	semicolons and colons

The Benefits and Structure of Inquiry

For conventions over which there is a general consensus—for example, with a few exceptions, such as e. e. cummings, writers begin sentences with capital letters—direct instruction may be our method of choice for its expediency. But over the years research has also pointed to other complex and messier ways that people acquire understanding and learn to apply it in different situations. Dewey says that "the pupil must learn what has meaning, what enlarges his horizon, instead of mere trivialities" ([1900] 1990, 78). We believe, of course, that the teaching of conventions as described previously is important, not trivial, because it leads to more comprehensible and therefore more powerful writing. But we also believe in the need to empower students to study language without our direct instruction, so that the ways they study it are lifelong, extending beyond the conventions they learn with us or the texts they see us write. We yearn to invite them to be active participants in the exploration of conventions, not just passive recipients of what passes as fact, so that they can retain what they've learned with us when they leave our classrooms behind.

This awareness of how people actually learn in lasting, sustainable ways lies at the heart of inquiry-based instruction. When we give students opportunities to conduct inquiry, they construct their own ideas about grammar, ideas they can take to their own writing processes and ultimately into the world. In their text *Spelling K–8*, Diane Snowball and Faye Bolton (1999) break down the inquiry approach into the following steps: inquiry; thinking; the forming and testing of hypotheses; the development of responsibility; the ability to reflect on and articulate what has been learned; and the ability to transfer knowledge and understanding from one situation to another. These steps are more linear on paper than they are in student performances, but they give us a framework to guide inquiry work.

We launch an inquiry by posing a question that teachers and their students will jointly explore. In a grammar inquiry, the questions can be as focused and precise as When and why do writers use commas? or something as broad and thought-provoking as Why do we need punctuation at all? For those who are new to the inquiry approach, though, it is often useful to base the inquiry around something that has been previously taught or is currently being taught through direct instruction in order to provide some extra support for students and teachers alike. For instance, if we have introduced ideas about paragraphing through direct instruction, we could return to them in an inquiry that looks more deeply at the art of paragraphing by exploring the question How do writers use paragraphs to help their readers understand more? or Why do writers choose to paragraph when they do? What effects are achieved by their choices? Teachers then ask students to revisit selected class texts to look for the ways different writers paragraph and to "notice what there is be noticed," as Maxine Greene says in *Releasing the Imagination* (1995, 125). Then we invite students to continue the exploration by finding additional usage examples in their independent reading.

Once students have collected a number of examples that are shared by the whole class on either charts or sentence strips, we ask them to try to group the examples into categories in order to begin to formulate ideas about the convention under question. They test these ideas against additional examples the students discover both in class and on their own, revising, reexamining, expanding, or clarifying their ideas as they continue the inquiry. Once their ideas are more substantial and solid, students may apply this newly gained knowledge to their own writing workshop work so that their writing reflects the kind of usage options they've explored in the inquiry.

A Sample Inquiry on the Use of Commas

To make this method more concrete, we offer the following example of an inquiry into commas based on the question of when and why writers use them. Like any kind of grammar instruction, we would not attempt to launch the inquiry until students felt invested in their writing. They must believe that *what* they write about matters—to themselves, to their classmates, to the community, to the world. They must feel a part of a writing community that supports and encourages risk. And once they've come to value their material, they must also be engaged in thinking about *how* they write in order to convey that material as powerfully, effectively, and movingly as they can.

We also need to have on hand a text that students have already had a chance to explore and enjoy as readers in order to support reading's highest goals: to help students see, as Anne Lamott says in her ode to the writing life, *Bird by Bird*, that "books are as important as almost anything else on earth . . . [They] help us understand who we are and how we are to behave. They show us what community and friendship mean; they show us how to live and die" (1994, 15). We don't, after all, read to learn about commas, though thinking about commas may help us understand whatever it is about life or human nature a writer wants us to see. So we look for texts that in some way speak to the heart and the human condition in addition to providing good examples of usage.

One text that we've used to launch an inquiry on commas with middle school students is Chaim Potok's story "Moon," from his collection *Zebra and Other Stories* (1998). The story is about a thirteen-year-old boy whose life of relative privilege and ease is forever changed when he meets a boy from Pakistan who was sold as a child to a carpet maker and forced to work as a slave. It encourages readers, as all good stories do, to reflect back on their own lives and to see the world with more empathetic eyes as a varied and complicated place. And it just so happens to be riddled with commas that are used for all kinds of purposes, as seen here in an excerpt from the first page:

> Moon Vinten, recently turned thirteen, was short for his age and too bony, too thin. He had a small pale face, dark angry eyes, and straight jet-black hair. A tiny silver ring hung from the lobe of his right ear, and a ponytail sprouted below the thick band at the nape of his neck and ran between his angular shoulder blades. The ponytail, emerging like a waterfall from the flat-combed dark hair, was dyed the clear blue color of a morning sky.
>
> Moon marched into the family den one autumn evening and announced to his parents that he wanted to build a recording studio for himself and his band.
>
> His parents, short, slender people in their late forties, had been talking quietly on the sofa. Moon's father, annoyed by his son's brusque interruption of the conversation, thought: First, those drums; then the earring and the ponytail. And now a *recording studio*? In a restrained tone, he asked, "What, exactly, does that involve?"
>
> "A big table, microphones, stands, extension cords, rugs or carpets for soundproofing, a mixing board," said Moon.
>
> "And how will you pay for all that?"

With the text on an overhead or printed on large paper and our inquiry's guiding question on the wall, we may first draw the students' attention to the number of commas in the passage—more than twenty in a rather short space. We can then ask them to consider the different occurrences of commas in the passage in order to begin to understand that commas serve different purposes. To assist their understanding, we might ask groups of students to write all the sentences in which commas appear on sentence strips, then try to group them according to any noticed similarities, and then compare the different findings and ideas of the groups. Thus, students might identify certain sentences where commas are used to separate items in a list (e.g., *small pale face, dark angry eyes,* or *a big table, microphones, stands . . .*), and others where commas are used in dialogue. In one eighth-grade classroom that studied this passage, students also pointed to the first and last sentences in the opening paragraph and noted how commas were used, as they described it, to "pack more into a sentence."

With some supportive modeling on the following day, these students also saw how those two sentences could be broken up into more than one. For instance,

> Moon Vinten, recently turned thirteen, was short for his age and too bony, too thin.

could become

> Moon Vinten recently turned thirteen. He was short for his age and too bony and thin.

while

> The ponytail, emerging like a waterfall from the flat-combed dark hair, was dyed the clear blue color of a morning sky.

could become

> The ponytail emerged like a waterfall from the flat-combed dark hair. It was dyed the clear blue color of a morning sky.

Students then compared the original sentence with the two that were created from it to see if they could articulate the difference between them in terms of how they sounded and felt to read in a way that once again underscores the connection between conventions and meaning and effect. Students' ability to do this with some degree of success is contingent, however, on how much experience they've had responding to writing in this more visceral and aesthetic way and how much they've heard us modeling it for them. For just as we teach students what good readers do when they read—visualize, connect, infer, make predictions—we need to teach them how writers read in a similar but slightly different way, one that writer and National Public Radio commentator Alan Cheuse describes as "that peculiar way that writers read, attentive to the particularities of language, to the technical turns and twists of scene-making and plot, soaking up numerous narrative strategies and studying the various approaches to the cave in the deep woods where the human heart hibernates" (2003, 28).

Author Jonathan Lethem speaks to this as well as he recalls a shift in his own reading:

> I [used to have] an insatiable appetite for complete narratives. I needed to know what happened. I'd fillet a novel of its story. Now I read more slowly, less to get to the end than for the pleasure of the sentences and paragraphs. Before, it was pure consumer frenzy. (in Miller 2004, 27)

As reading teachers we often feel successful when we see our students devouring books with the frenzy that Lethem describes. We want them to feel the pull of stories so keenly that they race to the end. But, particularly if we are writing teachers too, we don't want them to miss the delights of the journey in the rush to find out what happened. We want them to linger, to appreciate and savor a deft turn of phrase, a surprising metaphor, a nimble or smooth transition. We want them, in effect, to stop and smell the flowers that are found on every page because doing so will enrich their lives. And to do that we must model our own awareness of the pleasures and satisfactions to be found in texts at the level of paragraphs, sentences, and words.

In classes where students have had some prior practice with reading this way, students have been able to articulate their reactions to this excerpt from "Moon," with their responses falling into two basic camps. Some preferred Potok's writing, which they said seemed "to flow more" and not be so choppy, while others found Potok's sentences too busy and crowded and preferred the two-sentence class-revised versions. Through this articulation of the different effects, we can coauthor with our students a minilesson based on commas and choice, reflecting the usage that students have noticed and that they want to carry with them as writers.

To expand the inquiry, we can ask students to collect sentences from their independent reading or from other common classroom texts that they think fit—or don't fit—into the categories they began to develop with the whole-class excerpt. Thus they test their growing understanding of commas further, refine and define their categories more, and so come to more nuanced and complex understandings. They certainly need more examples, for instance, to reach a conclusion about why in the sentence *A tiny silver ring hung from the lobe of his right ear, and a ponytail sprouted below the thick band at the nape of his neck and ran between his angular shoulder blades,* there's a comma before the first *and* but not before the second. But through the careful study of similar sentences, they could come to see that the initial *and* connects two parts of the sentence that could actually stand alone, each as a separate sentence, while the part that follows the second *and* could not stand alone. And if they cannot reach this conclusion, even when looking at a wealth of examples, it is not inappropriate to jump in and let them know what the rule book says, provided they are given the opportunity to test the rule out on other examples themselves to see if it holds up or not. We can even name such a construct for our students once they have made this discovery, or have affirmed it through independent testing, saying that grammarians call this a compound-complex sentence, just as we might want to introduce the term *clause* instead of saying "part."

We believe, however, that students and teachers should be less concerned with identifying and naming grammatical constructs than with appreciating their effects. Beyond the world of the traditional classroom, it is not really critical to be able to name and distinguish a participial phrase, such as *emerging like a waterfall from the flat-combed dark hair,* from an appositive one, such as *short, slender people in their late forties*—though students might be able to identify that the former is constructed around a verb and the latter from a noun if they have enough examples to look at or if we alert them to it. But again, we believe that true literacy is based on understanding, not identification. The world, after all, abounds with literate people who cannot define the difference between a participle and an appositive but who can use them both effectively. And for real-world purposes, it is sufficient for students to see that they can add descriptive phrases set off by commas to make their writing richer, which they can do through the inquiry method and even more so through apprenticeship.

The Art of Apprenticeship

If direct instruction lets us explicitly convey grammatical rules as a way of handing over power, and inquiry sets up processes of collaborative and lifelong investigations of texts, with apprenticeship, we show students they can be more than functional writers. Apprenticeship is where we truly consider grammar as an art, relying on the way art provokes responses across differences of power, knowledge, and control.

When we begin to facilitate apprenticeship, we realize that there are ways in which published writers can do some of our teaching for us. Indeed, these writers can do teaching that is beyond us. Consider Jenny, an eighth-grade girl from the Lower East Side, studying Nabokov's famous sentence *My very photogenic mother died in a freak accident (picnic, lightning) when I was three:* she recast her first-draft sentence *My mother couldn't keep me when I was twelve* to *My not-so-loving mother felt unable (welfare, the projects) to keep me when I was twelve,* showing us the powerful intuitive response children have to art. If Jenny had read the whole novel, she would have been responding to it as literature. But she didn't; she responded to this sentence as a written art form. It is a response that is perhaps beyond the margins of our knowledge to predict, but that does not mean that we cannot try to stimulate it. Showing students how powerful writers use grammar as a transformative agent in the writing process is something we can do.

The process of apprenticeship is different from direct instruction and from inquiry in a few ways. In direct instruction, students see us make choices about conventions in our own writing, and they learn that the ability to make these choices is linked to one's power over language and fluency as a writer. In inquiry, students study the effect of grammar in a variety of texts, and they construct collaborative ideas about how grammar extends meaning. In apprenticeship, students emulate the styles and forms of writers who manipulate language in powerful ways. We model how to really study closely what writers are doing, using language that would help us imagine these tasks in our own writing.

Looking closely means showing students what it means to read when we pay attention at the sentence level. It means thinking about a single sentence as a mentor text that has many lessons to teach us. With Nabokov's sentence, we might start with noticing that it's written in the first person, that *My very photogenic mother* is the subject of the sentence, and that the subject is someone close to the narrator (and yet also at a bit of a distance, for the narrator says "photogenic," not "beautiful," which is, in some ways, a curious word choice). *Died in a freak accident* tells what happened to this person (it is the predicate). And the part in parentheses is like a secret narrative that gives us a whole story, a horrific event told in imagined images that enter our mind as we read that phrase, and that seems more shocking because it's sealed off, without comment, within those parentheses. And the final four words that come after this event bring us back to the narrator, and back even farther to a time when the narrator was younger. *My very photogenic mother died in a freak accident (picnic, lightning) when I was three.* So if we want to try to write a sentence like this one, that's the work we have to do. The most effective way is to emulate the form exactly, using similar phrases, which is what Jenny does. *My not-so-loving mother felt unable (welfare, the projects) to keep me when I was twelve.*

We will look more closely at what Jenny has done in Chapter 5, but for now it is critical to reiterate that if we want to facilitate apprenticeship, we ourselves have to savor language. We have to notice transformational grammar. We have to linger in texts. We read as potential writers and we collect. The texts we might emulate turn up often, though, simply in the stories that we read in school. If we return to the Chaim Potok text that we excerpted for our comma inquiry, we see that it makes a potentially powerful mentor text as well.

> Moon Vinten, recently turned thirteen, was short for his age and too bony, too thin. He had a small pale face, dark angry eyes, and straight jet-black hair. A tiny silver ring hung from the lobe of his right ear, and a ponytail sprouted below the thick band at the nape of his neck and ran between his angular shoulder blades. The ponytail, emerging like a waterfall from the flat-combed dark hair, was dyed the clear blue color of a morning sky.
>
> Moon marched into the family den one autumn evening and announced to his parents that he wanted to build a recording studio for himself and his band.
>
> His parents, short, slender people in their late forties, had been talking quietly on the sofa. Moon's father, annoyed by his son's brusque interruption of the conversation, thought: First, those drums; then the earring and the ponytail. And now a *recording studio*?

To read this closely, thinking how we might try some of what Potok does, we could look at the second sentence. *He had a small pale face, dark angry eyes, and straight jet-black hair.* We notice how it groups three groups of three words, each group a noun with two adjectives, so that there is a kind of rapid rush of words, a pause, another rapid rush, another pause. The commas create the pauses; they separate these phrases, and they also attach them. It's an uneasy sentence, which fits with Moon as an uneasy character. The commas are working, intimately conjoined with word choice, to give us an image of a character. The commas keep us lingering in that first paragraph, separating images, slowing us down, giving us a chance to visualize Moon, his skinniness, his punk wrapping, the way he has stylized an inability to fit in. Then in the second paragraph, we notice there are no commas. Here is Moon in action. He doesn't march into the family den, (pause) one autumn, nor does he want a recording studio, (pause) for himself and his band. He marches into the family den one autumn to demand a recording studio in one great burst. No commas. A one-sentence paragraph in the middle of other, more languorous paragraphs. In conjunction with the words, the form conveys a sense of urgency, speed, even desperate longing.

If we were to apprentice ourselves to Potok, we could consider using commas to separate and to link images and to slow the pace so the reader lingers inside the pictures the words create. We could alternate this kind of writing with rapid bursts of words with no commas, if we want to create a sudden sense of urgency or action. It is a seductive pleasure to study language this way. Don DeLillo writes that "working at sentences and rhythms is probably the most satisfying thing I do as a writer" (in Murray 1990, 160). When we study the sentences and rhythms of powerful writers, we begin to notice the conscious choices they make, and we can try these in our own writing.

Sometimes we hear teachers worry that students' voices will be blighted if they try to mimic the voices of other writers. But we believe that voice can shift and extend; that our voice is not limited to the ways of writing that we first come to; and that our students are, indeed, still students, apprentices, not yet masters, who will benefit and become stronger writers through exposure to different modes of expression. And just as Baroque painters copied earlier masterpieces to extend their skill and vision, so can studying writers. Goya's teacher was not a great painter. But Goya studied Velazquez, who was dead more than a hundred years before Goya picked up a brush. There is a lot to be learned from published writers; it is why, when asked to give students advice, writers most often say, "Read." Gary Paulsen says: "Read like a wolf eats!" (in Marcus 2000, 82). Feast and gorge yourself on words.

This kind of apprenticeship, the study of published writers and the attempt to emulate them, relies on students and teachers lingering in texts. Some writing is so subtle, and has so much possibility vibrating through it, that teachers and students need to spend much time pondering the text, more time than direct instruction would allow. And apprenticeship is not so teacher-led. We are doing individual and collaborative inquiry into the sentence, looking at how others imitate it, and having everyone try it. A productive way to facilitate this work is to read students the original sentence and articulate with them some of the things that make it powerful—reading it closely and parsing it for meaning—or starting with the first half of the sentence and letting them do the second half in partnerships. This is how it looks:

My very photogenic mother | died in a freak accident | (picnic, lightning) | when I was three.

describes someone and relation to narrator | tells what happened | gives secret story in images | tells when it was

In effect, we diagram the sentence for meaning, identifying how the different parts serve and enhance the whole instead of simply naming them; though once students have seen the function of the parts, we can introduce grammatical nomenclature, if we wish, returning to the sentence to parse it this way:

My very photogenic mother | died in a freak accident | (picnic, lightning) | when I was three.

subject—pronoun adverb adjective noun | predicate | (noun comma noun) | prepositional phrase describing age

It's worth taking time with these different parts, and the sentence as a whole, thinking about the effect of all this together, and we do so more in Chapter 5. But it's worth remembering here that if students struggle with this at first, they will become better at it with practice and modeling. Then we would move from the single sentence to showing students some writing examples that came in response to it. (Teachers can write their own, use examples from their students, or use the ones we've gathered, which we provide in Chapter 5.) Then students can conduct an inquiry into what they notice about the sentences and how they work. Then we can give them time to write several responses themselves, finishing by facilitating some reflection on what they learned as writers from this process, in terms of both strategies they used to mentor themselves and actual forms they may use in their future writing.

Mapping Curriculum to Support Grammar Instruction, Inquiry, and Apprenticeship

Inquiry and apprenticeship work takes more time than direct instruction, which is why this kind of work appears so rarely in secondary settings. With direct instruction, we give a minilesson and then the students work on their independent writing. Inquiry and apprenticeship work requires students to linger in texts and tasks. It is time well spent, but it does necessitate putting aside some time. And so when we consider our curriculum calendar, we may want to insert inquiry and apprenticeship work either as small independent studies in between publishing units or as embedded studies within larger units.

We like to plan inquiry work so that it supports our direct instruction and vice versa. Thus, if we plan to teach students paragraphing as revision in unit 1, and paragraphing again as a drafting strategy in unit 2, we might plan to also have an inquiry on the stylistic effect of paragraphing in unit 1 or unit 2. We could study the paragraph choices made by authors in a few texts. Thus we would support our direct instruction. In direct instruction, the students usually see our work as a model. In inquiry, they see other examples and they learn to study texts as potential writers. Inquiry can also be a form of word study, a way to inquire into the general ways that words work in English—their derivation, their common and uncommon endings—so that when we teach a lesson on writers choosing forms to achieve subject-verb agreement, students can support this lesson with inquiry work and a study of these forms.

In general, we plan apprenticeship work as a way to enliven and extend our instruction and to give alternatives to it. So, if we teach how to punctuate longer sentences so that students can learn to vary their sentence structure, we will probably also have an apprenticeship study of the artful sentence and how we can learn from published writers the unusual power of certain forms. This is apprenticeship work that enlivens and extends our instruction. Sometimes, we want to give alternatives. If we have been spending great effort teaching proper usage, for instance, we might plan to also look at how published writers sometimes break the rules. This keeps our grammar instruction from becoming dogmatic and routine and opens up the choices available to student writers as they do learn the rules. So our curriculum map might look like the following:

Unit 1

Inquiry: The purpose and effect of paragraphs

Unit 2

Apprenticeship: Playing with and extending subjects and predicates to say more

Inquiry: Fragments—their purpose and appropriateness

Unit 3

Inquiry: Pronoun forms

Inquiry: Verb forms

Unit 4

Inquiry: The effects of past and present verb tenses in prose

Apprenticeship: Switching verb tenses to achieve some of the effects published writers achieve

Unit 5

Inquiry: The effects of lists, and their commas, in prose and poetry

Unit 6

Inquiry: Apostrophes, pronouns, and meaning

Inquiry: Punctuation and poetry

Unit 7

Apprenticeship: The artful sentence

Inquiry and Apprenticeship: Breaking the rules

The Planning and the Reality

Sometimes, of course, our plans run aground on the rocky shores of real teaching. Our students need more support in certain areas; celebrations occur; things get in the way in sometimes beautiful and sometimes frustrating ways. But planning still helps us because we have a visible repertoire of instructional choices—a kind of grammatical toolkit from which we may grasp what seems best suited to the needs we face. As we assess our students, we may choose to shift some of the direct instruction lessons to small-group work. We may extend our inquiry work to the point where it replaces some direct instruction. We may convert a unit of study into a unit on apprenticeship. We may find ourselves moving more swiftly than these plans have indicated, or more slowly. Undoubtedly, however, we use our time more wisely when we have articulated curricular plans and when we work within a framework that is multifaceted and that gives attention to the diverse ways that writers learn to control language.

This is the framework we offer readers. It is a schema within which we hope teachers may embed instruction in conventions, artful grammar, and the deep study of language, using a variety of methods and enabling students in diverse ways. We close this chapter hoping that readers have a sense of

- how to plan and implement grammar lessons through direct instruction;
- how to insert inquiry in such a way that it supports and extends instruction;
- how to facilitate apprenticeship to enliven student writers;
- how to plan yearlong curriculum that includes direct instruction, inquiry, and apprenticeship; and
- how to use these plans as flexible and sustaining tools for instruction.

Please see A Curriculum Calendar of Direct Instruction Across the Writing Process on pages 44–45, and additional sample lessons on pages 46–48.

A Curriculum Calendar of Direct Instruction Across the Writing Process

	UNIT 1	UNIT 2	UNIT 3
FREEWRITING			**Lesson 1** (Ending Punctuation): Writers make choices about ending punctuation while writing. **Lesson 2** (Paragraphing): Fluent writers break their writing into chunks as they write.
DRAFTING		**Lesson 1** (Ending Punctuation): Writers make choices about ending punctuation as they draft. **Lesson 2** (Paragraphing): Writers make choices about inserting paragraphs while drafting.	**Lesson 3** (Subject and Predicate): Writers write complete sentences as they draft. **Lesson 4** (Fragments): Writers consider their genre and audience and make decisions about fragments as they draft.
REVISION	**Lesson 1** (Ending Punctuation): Writers make choices about ending punctuation as a revision strategy. **Lesson 2** (Paragraphing): Writers break their writing into smaller chunks during revision.	**Lesson 3** (Subject and Predicate): Writers compose complete sentences by including a subject and predicate. We revise our sentences. **Lesson 4** (Fragments): Writers understand that a fragment is not a sentence. We consider the appropriateness and effectiveness of fragments in revision.	**Lesson 5** (Subject-Verb Agreement): Writers revise their writing so that subject and verb agree, and we learn singular and plural forms of nouns, pronouns, and verbs to do this. **Lesson 6** (Subject and Object): Writers understand subject and object in order to use the proper form of pronouns and *who/whom*. We revise our writing to use proper forms of pronouns and *who/whom*. We revise our writing to use proper forms.

A Curriculum Calendar of Direct Instruction Across the Writing Process, cont'd.

UNIT 4	UNIT 5	UNIT 6	UNIT 7
Lesson 3 (Subject and Predicate): Fluent writers mostly compose in complete sentences when writing prose. **Lesson 4** (Fragments): Writers, if they use fragments, do so knowingly, purposefully, and sparingly.	**Lesson 5** (Subject-Verb Agreement): Writers practice subject-verb agreement as they write. **Lesson 6** (Subject and Object): Writers try to use the proper forms of pronouns and *who/whom* as they write.	**Lesson 7** (Verb Tense): Writers make choices about verb tense as they write, and they strive to use verb endings and forms consistent with their choice. **Lesson 8** (Punctuating Dialogue): Writers learn to punctuate dialogue properly, and we punctuate as needed while writing.	**Lesson 9** (Commas in Lists): Writers know how commas separate items in a list and use commas this way as we write. **Lesson 10** (Using Commas and Conjunctions): Writers know how to write longer sentences by joining complete sentences with a comma and a conjunction. We strive to vary our sentences this way when writing.
Lesson 5 (Subject-Verb Agreement): Writers practice subject-verb agreement as they draft. **Lesson 6** (Subject and Object): Writers try to use the proper forms of pronouns, and *who/whom* as they draft.	**Lesson 7** (Verb Tense): Writers make choices about verb tense as they draft and they try to maintain verb endings consistent with their tense choice. **Lesson 8** (Punctuating Dialogue): Writers learn to punctuate dialogue properly, and we punctuate as needed while drafting.	**Lesson 9** (Commas in Lists): Writers learn how commas separate items in a list and use commas this way as we draft. **Lesson 10** (Using Commas and Conjunctions): Writers learn to write longer sentences by joining complete sentences with a comma and a conjunction. We can vary our sentences this way while drafting.	**Lesson 11** (Apostrophes): Writers understand how apostrophes signify possessive forms and contractions, and we strive to use these forms to convey meaning as we draft. **Lesson 12** (Semicolons and Colons): Writers understand that the semicolon and colon can be interesting ways to join sentences. We use them these ways as we draft.
Lesson 7 (Verb Tense): Writers make choices about verb tense as a revision strategy and they maintain the tense of their choice by learning and checking their verb endings. **Lesson 8** (Punctuating Dialogue): Writers learn to punctuate dialogue properly, and we punctuate as needed in revision.	**Lesson 9** (Commas in Lists): Writers learn how commas separate items in a list, and we revise our writing to include them. **Lesson 10** (Using Commas and Conjunctions): Writers learn to write longer sentences by joining complete sentences with a comma and a conjunction. We can revise our writing for greater sentence variety.	**Lesson 11** (Apostrophes): Writers study how apostrophes signify possessive forms and contractions, and we revise our writing to use these forms to convey meaning. **Lesson 12** (Semicolons and Colons): Writers learn that the semicolon and colon can be interesting ways to join sentences. We study their usage and try them in revision.	

Some Other Sample Lessons

A SECOND LESSON IN ENDING PUNCTUATION
*Writers Make Choices About Ending
Punctuation as They Draft*

Connection and Invitation

So when we were revising our last pieces, we checked that the first letter of the first word of a new sentence was capitalized, and we considered the choices writers make for ending punctuation. We realized that there are three choices for ending punctuation—a period, a question mark, and an exclamation point—and we began to make more effective decisions about how to end each sentence in our piece as we revised. Today I want to teach you that writers don't wait for revision to consider how they will begin and end their sentences.

Teaching Point

Writers use capital letters to start sentences as they draft, and they make significant choices about ending punctuation even as they are drafting. Watch me do this work. Try to watch in such a way that you can describe what I'm doing as a writer. OK, I'm moving out of my notebook today into drafting.

I'm writing an essay this time about how the urge to belong sometimes pushes us to do destructive things. I'm just at this point in my draft:

> Sometimes, in the urge to belong, we hurt ourselves and people close to us because we are too afraid to speak up. I was too afraid to speak to my mother about the alligator thing. Or maybe I was too embarrassed. And so we never spoke about it and I missed the chance to find out what she would say or how she would help me.

Let me see, now that I've written a few sentences, I'm going to reread them before going on. I'm rereading that first sentence and thinking that a period works for that—it makes the tone clear and steady, which is good for this statement. Now, I could put an exclamation point after this first sentence. Then it sounds more emphatic. And I could put a question mark after the third sentence—that would give a sense of uncertainty. I kind of like the tone of that because it gives the essay more of a tone of uncertainty and discovery. Let me read them in different ways.

Active Engagement and Reflection

Talk to your partner about how you would choose to punctuate these sentences and why. Then let's talk about how you made these decisions even this early in the drafting process and what it may mean for the piece.

Or

Talk to your partner for a minute about how writers may decide on ending punctuation as we draft. How do we do this and why?

Link to Ongoing Work and Writing Practices

So whenever you are drafting, as you write, reread your writing and make careful choices about your ending punctuation. You make discoveries this way, as you write, and you make choices that affect your draft.

A THIRD LESSON IN ENDING PUNCTUATION
Writers Develop Habits of Mind

Connection and Invitation

Last time we considered ending punctuation, we realized that writers reread their sentences as they are drafting, and they consider the choices they are making about ending punctuation as they draft. Today I want to teach you that writers don't wait until they draft to punctuate their sentences effectively.

Teaching Point

Writers make choices as they freewrite, both as a way to develop their writing fluency and to simply make it a habit of mind to always write clearly and purposefully. Watch me do this work. I'm going to freewrite in front of you. Try to watch in such a way that you can describe what I'm doing as I write.

I'm freewriting about playing tackle tag in the summer on our neighbor's lawn. I was reading Sandra Cisneros's story "Hips," and it made me think about games played by children on our street. I'm not sure what it will become yet—maybe I'll use it if I write about Cisneros's story. So, I'm writing about playing tackle tag on summer evenings in fourth grade. All the kids on our block played. Lisa played, and also Chris, this incredibly fast and beautiful sixth-grade boy. Here are the first few sentences of my freewrite:

Chris was often "it." Chris's hair was yellow, his eyes were blue, his bare arms and legs were brown. The tag in tackle tag consisted of being knocked to the ground. When his hard sixth-grade arms wrap around your fourth-grade body, holding you just off the ground, it is like nothing you ever knew before.

OK, I'm going to reread and make some choices as a writer before I keep writing. I'm looking at that last sentence, and I'm thinking that I could use an exclamation point. Then it would sound like this [read it with more overt excitement]:

When his hard sixth-grade arms wrap around your fourth-grade body, holding you just off the ground, it is like nothing you ever knew before!

Hmm, I'm just starting this piece, and I think I want it to be reflective. I'm thinking I may turn it into a vignette that I can either publish or use when I write about Cisneros's story. And I like the way in her piece, as the children jump rope and talk about their bodies, they seem unaware of the significance of what they are saying. Let me read it again.

Active Engagement and Reflection

I'm going to write a bit more. Talk with your partner about how you might punctuate these sentences and what your choices might mean for what this freewrite might become.

When you felt Chris's arms around you, holding you just off the ground, you wondered what would it feel like if this weren't tag. I escaped Chris the first time, but only by a little. Then Lisa ran in between Chris and me. Lisa had brown hair and slim legs and was a very fast runner. Chris caught Lisa first.

Or

What are some ways we can develop punctuation habits? Based on the work you just saw me do, talk with your partner about your ideas.

Or

Talk with your partner and get ready to share ideas on what you will do differently when you freewrite now.

Link to Ongoing Work and Writing Practices

So whenever you are writing, you can be practicing and developing habits of mind that reflect powerful writing practices. One of these habits is the habit of making significant punctuation choices as you write.

Teaching Usage
Punctuation, Conventions, Style

"I really do not know that anything has ever been more exciting than diagramming sentences," says Gertrude Stein in her essay "Poetry and Grammar" (1967, 126). Few of us share Gertrude Stein's exciting memories. Most of us, when we remember our own instruction in English grammar, if we recollect it at all, recall worksheets, and parsing, and menacing forms such as dangling participles, split infinitives, and run-on sentences. What did they dangle from, how were they split, where did they run to? These feel like things we should know, but distressingly, at least in our case, we can't actually remember *how* to diagram a sentence, or why an infinitive cannot be split, if indeed it cannot be. We wonder if we need to go back and study Latin before we start teaching English. In a state akin to panic, we may bring out the red pens and workbooks, prepared to drill students in the horrors of comma splices and the pitfalls of fragments. And chillingly, at the back of our minds lurks the uneasy suspicion that we won't recognize a comma splice or know when it is a problem.

That grammar may be an unfamiliar and intimidating subject for teachers as well as students is worth acknowledging. There is judgment linked with usage—correct use of punctuation, form, and word choice—and so it is safer to avoid performances in which our knowledge of usage will be highly visible. We find ourselves recasting sentences to avoid a potential blunder. Unsure whether it should be *He's the one who everyone chooses first for his or her team* or *He's the one whom everyone chooses first for his or her team,* we say instead *He's the one everyone chooses first for his or her team.* (It is *whom.* We choose *him/whom.*) Teaching grammar is treading dangerous waters.

We have to teach usage for two reasons. One is that knowledge of usage is fundamentally linked to power and access to power. In "The Silenced Dialogue," Lisa Delpit describes how parents and teachers of color felt estranged from the progressive atmosphere of writing process because they felt it did not serve their children well. One parent in Delpit's text says starkly: "White kids learn how to write a decent sentence. Even if they don't teach them in school, their parents make sure they get what they need" (1995, 16). We might argue that this parent's use of *white* is monumental and really she means white-literate-middle-class. But why argue? Delpit gives voice to parents who feel that some educational goals, particularly the teaching of voice over conventionality, are not serving their children well. Even if we disagree initially, even if we long to defend the purity and long-term efficacy of writing process, how can we not listen? Delpit asserts that the codes of grammar are among the codes of what she calls the "culture of power." She argues that "if you are not already a participant in the culture of power, being told explicitly the rules of that culture makes acquiring power easier" (24). As white teachers ourselves, teachers working in urban high-poverty schools populated with high percentages of students of color, this argument took us aback and made us reconsider what lessons we include in teaching writing and how our choices might mean we are holding onto power rather than sharing it.

Delpit makes a forceful statement about writing process and the way that, as it sometimes plays out in the classroom, it may be unintentionally strengthening the status quo of power. She says:

> Many liberal educators hold that the primary goal for education is for children to become autonomous, to develop fully who they are in the classroom setting without having arbitrary, outside standards forced upon them. This is a very reasonable goal for people whose children are already participants in the culture of power and who have already internalized its codes.
>
> But parents who don't function within that culture often want something else. It's not that they disagree with the former aim, it's just that they want something more. They want to ensure that the school provides their children

with discourse patterns, interactional styles, and spoken and written language codes that will allow them success in larger society. (29)

And so our first reason for teaching usage is that this instruction is one way to transfer power. The way we talk about grammar matters, then. It will make a difference how we talk about hierarchies of language, questions of access and purpose, and the different beauties and power of various language decisions. The language decisions students make in writing a song or a poem may differ from those made in writing essays or letters, depending on their audience and how they want to interact with this audience.

Gloria Ladson-Billings, in *The Dreamkeepers: Successful Teachers of African American Children*, describes what she calls culturally relevant pedagogy as pedagogy that respects the diverse cultures present at school and home, that gives room for these to flourish, but that at the same time has "teachers and students engage in a collective struggle against the status quo" (1994, 117). These seem difficult requirements at first, to both respect and value diverse cultures and act to change power inequalities in the literacy classroom. But writing workshop and grammar work conjoin to partially fulfill these obligations, in the way that students have myriad opportunities to write about their lives while learning the ways that control of language is linked to power. In this way we can follow Ladson-Billings's tenets that "students' real-life experiences are legitimized as they become part of the 'official' curriculum" and that "students are apprenticed in a learning community rather than taught in an isolated and unrelated way" (117).

We convey to students that academic English, or standard written English, is currently the language of power in this country, and that some doors, such as those giving entry to many places of higher education, certain jobs, institutions, and even relationships, may open only to those who have control of usage. In this way, we embed usage as one of the many discourses of power that education helps us recognize, master, and perhaps set aside, but this choice will be dictated by personal or artistic reasons rather than educational limits. We do this with some hesitation. We worry that in acknowledging the language of power, we are complicit in adherence to it. We worry about what Tom Romano (1995) has implied, that some students are better served by other linguistic options than standard English because they will have stronger voices in other patterns. But we hearken to Delpit's plea that "to act as if power does not exist is to ensure that the power status quo remains the same," and so we name grammar as one of the many codes of power, and one way we teach it is as part of the knowledge students and teachers need to share to equalize opportunity.

We are also concerned with student voice. We want students to have voices in many communities, and we want those voices to be both powerful and individual. We don't want to teach only toward conformity. This concern is a second compelling reason to teach usage. Grammar can be a transformative agent in writing and a way to strengthen and extend voice. It enlarges the writer's ability to convey meaning. It gives clarity and beauty to our words. It teaches discipline. Taught seductively, it constrains in ways that are stimulating, it lures us into new spaces even as it seems to fence us in.

Ultimately, knowledge of grammar is knowledge of how to put words and punctuation next to each other in fluid and consequential ways. There is power here, and there is also art. And so we desire to offer our students knowledge of the power of grammar and also of its beauty. It is rather like a love affair with a difficult lover. We move through stages of mastery and submission, until we achieve a partnership that satisfies. Don Murray writes that "each day the writer returns to word play—clause play, sentence play, paragraph play— constantly surprised that this old lover is forever young, forever the provider of surprise, delight, and insight" (1990, 159). With knowledge, with ease, eventually comes pleasure.

The Knowledge Teachers Need

The power and love of grammar that will flourish in our classrooms starts with us. Teaching students modern usage comes more readily when we are at ease with it ourselves and understand how it informs our own writing. We've found that the best way to gain this knowledge is to create our own examples for everything we are going to teach *and everything we want to understand better*. It is the only way to truly feel how these rules apply to writers in the act of composing. Some of the rules of usage are not intuitive, and we grasp their usefulness only when we struggle with them ourselves as writers—it takes more effort, that is, than the recognition that comes with reading.

What follows is a primer on usage that asks the reader to compose a personal catalog of examples to accompany the ones presented here. This primer embraces the knowledge of usage with which we most commonly find ourselves composing sentences. Starting with the vast descriptions of usage found in Fowler and Fowler's *The King's English* ([1906] 2002), Amis's *The King's English: A Guide to Modern Usage* (1997), Strunk and White's *The Elements of Style* (2000), Weaver's *Teaching Grammar in Context* (1996), and Truss's *Eats, Shoots and Leaves* (2003), we have pruned, and sorted, and organized what we consider to be the most important understandings of usage, and we have put them in an order that we think leads to effective writing. There is more in our collection than Strunk and White deem necessary, and far less than is discussed by Fowler, and we try to use ordinary language as much as possible. We don't teach with negative examples; too often, as soon as we present them, they become what students remember, and so we present only correct usage, always linking grammar to power, meaning, and voice.

We offer this catalog for teachers as writers and for student writers. For teachers, we hope the experience of studying, trying, and adding personal examples to this primer will strengthen a more individual understanding of usage and foster a better position from which to plan and teach. Those workbooks have been deadly not only for children but also for us. "What happened to punctuation?" asks Truss (2003, 13). It was lying dormant in worksheets, unable to breathe or do its work. We need to release punctuation from the muck of worksheets. We need to know and have words for how punctuation enlivens writing, how it shapes meaning, how it matters to us as people who write and teach writing. We need to say what punctuation does for us and what it can do for the student writers we teach. We need words, and we need examples.

The Power of Story: Composing Examples Within a Narrative

Usage is meaningless as a series of isolated rules or exercises. If we want students to care about grammar, we have to demonstrate its power. One way is to talk about the culture of power, as Delpit does, and we do this when we speak of why learn grammar at all. And then we want to show the power grammar gives to writers as they write. We choose to demonstrate its power through story. Story helps students attach meaning to difficult concepts. Story carries our students with us into new explorations. Story is seductive, it has the potential for beauty, for meaning, for surprise; story is the finest companion we have as teachers. It is not accidental that the first book on punctuation ever read by people other than student or professional writers is Lynne Truss's *Eats, Shoots and Leaves* (2003), which tells the story of punctuation through a series of anecdotes. It has sold hundreds of thousands of copies, to mainstream audiences, because it tells a good story.

As teachers of reading as well as writing, we know the thrall of story. John Gardner describes it as a "vivid dream" that pulls us in and seduces us:

> We read a few words at the beginning of the book or the particular story, and suddenly we find ourselves seeing not words on a page but a train moving through Russia, an old Italian crying, or a house battered by rain. We read on— dream on—not passively but actively, worrying about the choices the characters have to make, listening in panic for some sound behind the fictional door, exulting in characters' successes, bemoaning their failures . . . the dream engages us heart and soul. (1984, 30)

We see students surrender themselves to story and then emerge ready to talk, but to talk from a different knowledge base than the one they had before they encountered the story. Literary theorist Eve Sedgwick describes this almost revelatory quality of story also, when she describes "the inexplicit compact by which novel-readers voluntarily plunge into worlds that strip them, however temporarily, of the painfully acquired cognitive maps of their ordinary lives" (1990, 97). There is magic in story. Story takes us out of the schoolroom, out of the neighborhood, out of the family and friendship circles that cherish and constrain us. It seems one of the few almost universal conditions of humanity: to be human is to long for stories.

We perhaps underestimate how powerful it is to tell stories habitually in our lessons and to have stories that live in our classrooms as common narratives. We particularly like to use what we call unsafe stories, that is, stories that demonstrate inequities of power, knowledge, or control or the force of acknowledged and unacknowledged desires. Unsafe stories help us show writing as a way to consider and construct identity. And these models often help students choose more meaningful subjects and purposes for writing. For example, the anecdote we told to demonstrate our lessons in Chapter 2, is such a story:

I remember when I was in sixth grade, it was so important to have an alligator shirt—the real thing, an Izod, with a little alligator on the left breast, and you could only get them at one store in our town, this store called Papagallo that was much more expensive than JC Penney and much much more expensive than Sears or Kmart, and the shirts were $65 which was a lot for a short sleeve cotton shirt in 1977. And I'm sure there were kids in my school who didn't wear alligator shirts, and maybe didn't even care about alligator shirts, but I didn't know any, and in the group of kids whom I thought of as friends, it seemed very important to have one, at least. Lisa and Christina each had about a dozen, and they were the most popular girls in school.

My mom brought a shirt home for me one night from Sears, but it had an elephant on the pocket, and she couldn't understand why I burst into tears, tears of sorrow that we didn't have more money and tears of shame that it mattered to me. I didn't wear the shirt with the elephant, but I heard Christina making fun in the cafeteria of kids who had fake shirts, and how if you couldn't have the real thing, you shouldn't try to pretend to be rich. All the kids at the table agreed those shirts were "gay." That weekend, in Papagallo, in the little cubicle dressing room, I tried on one of those Izod shirts which we couldn't afford, there was no way we had the money for it, and I ripped off the alligator *and the label* and put them in my pocket. Then I took them home and sewed them on the shirt my mom had given me and I sat next to Lisa at lunch the next day.

It is productive to imagine the many possible grammar lessons, and other writing lessons, we can demonstrate with this story. We've found that students *stay with us* in the grammar lessons because they are invested in the story and in the meanings that reside in it. We see it in how students lean forward once we talk about the story, we see it in how they have access to the lesson because they have access to the world of the story, we see it in how they talk about possibility and consequence as if the story were real to them. We see how story makes the grammar seem real.

In the context of a minilesson, students have offered possible grammatical revisions, such as taking the last phrase—*I sat next to Lisa at lunch the next day*—and making it one sentence, and its own paragraph, for dramatic emphasis. One seventh grader said that would show how the narrator sits with Lisa but is really still all alone. As we consider adding sentences to the narrative, as the demonstration part of the minilessons, students consider the punctuation seriously because they are considering how it will affect the meaning of the sentence and the story as a whole. And so in a lesson on punctuation choice, they debated fiercely whether, if we added: *I sat in the dressing room holding the seam ripper and wondered what would happen if I were caught,* we should end that sentence with a period, an exclamation, or a question mark. Most wanted it to say: *I sat in the dressing room holding the seam ripper. What would happen if I were caught?* One fifth grader said almost ferociously, break it up, you'll have to, see how you can't just keep it as one sentence if you want to make it sound like you are really worried? The students were worried about voice, they were worried for the story. That's what unsafe stories can do for us—they invite, they entice, they risk.

Where do we find the stories we will use? We don't, as teachers, have to be professional writers. But we can be people who write, and just as our students' lives are worth writing about, so are ours. In general, we find that stories that are particularly compelling in the classroom include

- stories of childhood
- narratives of desire and temptation
- stories about the urge to belong
- moments of choice

And so these unsafe stories are ones that are about identity, about risk, and about choice, and about the perplexing presence of forces in our lives over which we have, as yet, little control or knowledge. As we search for these stories, we find they are often hiding in places where these issues reside:

- the cafeteria
- the gym
- recess and after-school play
- lockers, the hallways
- friendship circles
- family relations and expectations
- clothes, the stuff we wear and carry

We are not afraid to fictionalize; we strive for the story to sound true on the page. Our allegiance is to the emotional truth of whatever we're writing about, not to the facts as they actually happened or our spotty, unreliable memories. So we generate details that would be impossible to recall, we monumentalize events that are only half remembered, we do the work that writers do in telling a compelling story. And when we talk about these stories in the classroom, we are talking about life as it is shown in story.

And so even, or especially, when we compose grammatical examples, we compose within a compelling story. In each sentence we compose as a teaching example, we also compose more of the narrative and we enhance the voice that comes through in the story. The narratives we create in the classroom wrap themselves around our grammar work, so we choose and compose them strategically and lovingly. We ask ourselves what stories we want to play with as we play with commas and semicolons. Some things we know: stories of desires, the yearning to know more, or the achievement of longed-for experiences make powerful classroom stories. Youth adore Harry Potter because we all long for powers that would let us transcend everyday constraints. We know, too, that stories of youth are compelling and generative in the classroom, and so we tell stories of childhood.

The particular story that follows tells of the very beginnings of inexperienced love felt by a fourth-grade girl for a sixth-grade boy. It was composed for older students, ones who have felt these passions already and who therefore recognize their meaning and potential even as they struggle with grammatical choices. These examples supported our work with adolescents, eighth and ninth graders for whom the study of grammar becomes especially difficult because it can be humiliating, part of the knowledge they should have by now but don't. And so here, we carry adolescents through punctuation and sentence structure by carrying them into summer evenings of tackle tag, transcending the schoolroom in order to transform this academic study. We are doing our best, in other words, to make grammar pleasurable by creating a narrative of preadolescent experience that will carry students through the work willingly and even eagerly. In *Romantic Understanding*, Kieran Egan urges us to engage adolescents with knowledge by engaging their romantic understanding. Romance, writes Egan, "involves an urge beyond our everyday lot, an urge to transcend the conventions that surround us, to remake the world closer to our heart's desire" (1990, 111). The longings of youth to know more, to feel more, may seem like a strange partner for the study of commas and clauses. But we can intrigue students with the control of language by showing how it is one way to give voice to stories we want to tell and hear.

Figure out what's compelling material for the students you teach. Or consider what story *you* want to tell, remembering what E.B. White says: that "writing is an act of faith, not a trick of grammar." He adds, "Your whole duty as a writer is to please and satisfy yourself, and the true writer always plays to an audience of one" (Strunk and White 2000, 84). It's the act of storytelling that gives heart to teaching. The story we write can be simple; this story of tackle tag is hardly more than a vignette. Have faith that the small moments of our lives are worth writing about. Compose sentence by sentence. And so, pens at the ready, we open our study.

Beginning and Ending Punctuation

One of the primary rules of usage is that we capitalize the first word of a sentence. This usage seems so commonplace that few texts on style include it. We do teach it, though, for several reasons. Primarily, it gives us a way to launch a story, but it also lets us reteach in the context of composing. We show students how we make the capital letters especially legible so that the reader can clearly understand our meaning. This helps us make this a lesson on fluent writing practices. And it helps us as well instill in our students an abiding respect for the alphabet, a love for what Eudora Welty describes as "all the wizardry of letter, initial, and word" (1983, 10). We write plenty of sentences, composing enough to invite students into our story:

> Writers capitalize the first letter of the first word of a sentence so the reader knows it is a new sentence. At the end of a sentence, we put ending punctuation (a period, an exclamation point, or a question mark). If we are writing by hand, then writers make an effort to be especially legible with capitals and ending punctuation so that readers recognize their sentences.
>
> In summer all the kids on our block played tackle tag. Chris, David, Billy, Karen, Michael, Ben, Amy, Lisa, and me. We played every night from right after supper until it was dark and we heard our mothers calling, whistling, or ringing bells.

> Sometimes we played in our backyard, where there was a treehouse to hide in and a garage to run around. But mostly we played on Mrs. Terhaar's lawn, where there was no place to get away, and the sidewalk, the street corner, and the driveway edged us in.

Modern English usage also demands ending punctuation. We offer this as a significant moment of choice for the writer:

> Writers make choices about ending punctuation to achieve certain effects. Ending punctuation choices include the period, the exclamation point, and the question mark.
>
> A period achieves a neutral effect; it lets the reader create meaning from the words only.
>
> It made a difference if you were fast. [Implies: Hmm, OK, we'll learn more soon.]
>
> It made a difference to Chris. Chris was the fastest runner, and the most beautiful too.
>
> An exclamation point implies a sense of overt excitement.
>
> It made a difference if you were fast! [Implies: Wowza! You know what I mean!]
>
> It made a difference to Chris! Chris was the fastest runner, and the most beautiful too!
>
> A question mark implies a question or wonderment, bewilderment, or anxiety.
>
> It made a difference if you were fast? [Implies: Why? Really? How? Are you sure?]
>
> It made a difference to Chris? Chris was the fastest runner, and the most beautiful too?

We play with our punctuation choices in the lesson and then we add our revisions to our narrative. We choose the period here, as it sustains the tone of a story that is still developing and is still cautious in its tone. Despite being seemingly mundane, periods are often the most effective punctuation choice. In this story, the exclamation point would invite the reader in too much, would imply a kind of complicit and overt excitement that we don't want to build yet—we want our tone to be more reflective and measured. In the same way, a question mark would imply that the narrator is surprised by the story, whereas in this case the narrator knows the story but is still discovering the meaning of it. The period is just right. It offers just enough stability. Ending punctuation is directly related to the tone of the sentence and thus to the overall tone of this part of the piece.

Another note about the exclamation point: when we demonstrate, we try to avoid choosing it except in dialogue. Student writers have a penchant for exclamation points. Fowler and Fowler claim: "The exclamation-mark must not be used . . . we feel that the writer is indeed lost in admiration of his own wit or impressiveness. But this use is mainly confined to lower-class authors" ([1906] 2002, 255). Clearly usage is judged in complicated and unpleasant ways that support Delpit's claims about a culture of power. And while we, as readers, are not immune to the power of a well-placed exclamation mark, particularly when it hints at something more than just excitement, we tend to follow Strunk and White's advice: "Do not attempt to emphasize simple statements by using a mark of exclamation" (2000, 34).

Paragraphing

The lesson we offer next is one on paragraphing. As soon as writers are writing a few sentences, it is helpful to consider how to chunk and arrange these sentences effectively. Strunk and White advise: "Make the paragraph the unit of composition" (2000, 15). They add: "Enormous blocks of print look formidable to readers, who are often reluctant to tackle them" (17). There is no usage rule about when to paragraph, but there are many possibilities that we can offer writers.

> Writers break long chunks of writing into paragraphs. Writers often insert new paragraphs when
>
> > a new character enters a narrative
> > the setting changes

> the time changes
> someone new is speaking
> the writer wants to introduce or emphasize a new idea
> the writer wants to separate and emphasize different sections or subtopics
> the writer wants to create a dramatic effect by isolating a sentence or chunk of
>   sentences

We decide in this piece to start a new paragraph with *It made a difference if you were fast*, to introduce and emphasize the start of some tension and also because we are moving to Chris, which is a new focus in our story. We stay with Chris, holding to him as the focus of this paragraph. Gertrude Stein writes that "paragraphs are emotional." She adds, "Paragraphs are emotional not because they express an emotion but because they register or limit an emotion" (1967, 54). When we paragraph, we hold something all together and inside at once. And so we have an opportunity, here, to hold Chris, to tuck into this paragraph all that was magical about him. We make a whole paragraph now, all about Chris:

> It made a difference if you were fast. Chris was the fastest runner, and the most beautiful too. The tag in tackle tag consisted of being knocked to the ground. Chris was often "it." Chris's hair was yellow, his eyes were blue, his bare arms and legs were brown. When his hard sixth-grade arms wrapped around your fourth-grade body, holding you just off the ground, it was like nothing you ever knew before. It was something undomesticated.

The gorgeous thing about paragraphs is how they implicitly wrap themselves around what's inside them, making a container that keeps everything inside intimate and forever conjoined. The paragraph holds Chris, but also the narrator and the narrator's longings, and a single moment on a summer evening, a moment somehow contained now, named and held. Paragraphs are emotional.

The Sentence and the Fragment

Gertrude Stein claims that sentences are not emotional, but we disagree. The sentence is the stuff of the story, and in every sentence resides a small story. We start our examination of sentences by looking at what's inside the sentence, teaching subject and predicate—what makes a sentence. All complete sentences (and clauses) have a *subject*, which is a noun or a pronoun, followed by a *predicate*, which is a verb or a verb phrase. While we tend to avoid technical terminology as much as possible, we teach subject and predicate because they are intrinsic to constructing complete sentences. We preface this teaching by reviewing the terms *noun, pronoun, verb, adjective,* and *adverb,* so that we'll be ready to extend our subjects and predicates. We use familiar words from the story to show how we are using all these parts of speech already in our writing, and we study the role they play in giving meaning and evoking mood in the story. For example:

Noun: The name of a person, place, thing, idea (*summer, kids, block, tackle tag, lawn, street-corner, driveway, Chris, hair, eyes, arms, legs, body, ground, something*)

Pronoun: A word that stands for a noun (*we, he, you, us, his, your*)

Verb: A word showing action or state of being (*played, run, knock, wrap, holding*)

Adjective: A word that describes or modifies a noun (*dark, fast, fastest, beautiful, yellow, blue, bare, brown, hard, undomesticated*)

Adverb: A word that describes or modifies a verb, an adjective, or an adverb (*most*)

Just listing these words lets us roll them over our tongues, thinking about what they do in the story. Roll out the nouns and you roll out the explicit stuff of the story—it is a story of arms and legs and bodies and lawns. And Chris. Move to the pronouns and we get the unnamed narrator and more of the players. The verbs bring them all together, tangle them up in action. The adjectives let us in on how the narrator sees it all, the visions in the eye and the dreams in the heart, the *yellow* hair, the *blue* eyes, the *undomesticated* feelings inside a fourth grader. The adverbs give emphasis only where it is most needed. Chris is the *most* beautiful.

When we move from parts of speech to the parts of the sentence, it helps us explain these terms when the subject of our sentence is someone whom students recognize as the subject of the story. We ask: Whom is the story all about? It's all about Chris. If Chris is the subject, what he does is the predicate.

A sentence includes a subject and a predicate. If the subject is *Chris*, the predicate is *what Chris does*. The subject can also include words that describe Chris. The predicate can also include words related to what Chris does. A sentence or clause always includes subject plus verb or verb phrase.

Subject: Chris (and how he is described)   *Predicate:* **What Chris does**

Chris **was twelve.**
Chris **was truly heartbreakingly beautiful.**
Chris **was twelve and beautiful.**
Chris **was the fastest runner on our block.**
Chris **caught everyone when we played tackle tag.**
Chris, who was the fastest runner on our block, **caught everyone one night.**
Chris, who was twelve and beautiful, **caught everyone one night.**
Chris, who when he was twelve was the fastest runner and truly heartbreakingly beautiful, **caught everyone when we played tackle tag.**

We compose Chris as the subject of the story and of the sentence. It's easier for students to grasp the relationship of subject and predicate if they too ask: Who is the subject of my story, and what is something this person does? Our goal is to compose complete sentences. Subject plus verb or verb phrase. *Chris was fast.* We can say a bit more; we can add what Strunk and White call "related words" after the subject or verb. We don't need to introduce complicated terms for this work; we just demonstrate how writers realize they can say more in one sentence if they choose, and we can do so, employing some of those adjectives and adverbs. *Chris was truly heartbreakingly beautiful when he was twelve.*

Sometimes, we make things more visible by showing not only what they are but what they are not. It is useful to demonstrate fragments in comparison to sentences that have a subject and a predicate. Fragments do not. A fragment can be merely a noun, or a noun and an adjective, or merely a verb. Writers use fragments judiciously (or perhaps some writers do this injudiciously and wildly, but we present it as a carefully judged action since we are aware how hostile some educators are to fragments). Because we believe in their effectiveness when used judiciously in certain genres, we do include a lesson on fragments, or the "clipped sentence," as Strunk and White name this form.

> Writers understand that a fragment is not a sentence. It doesn't have both a subject and a predicate. Fragments are used with an awareness of genre and audience. Writers understand that some audiences, such as academic publications and graders of standardized tests, are hostile to all fragments.
>
> On the other hand, writers sometimes use fragments powerfully, to achieve a certain effect such as a rapid pace or an emphasis on detail. The last three sentences in this paragraph are not, in fact, full sentences; they are deliberate fragments:
>
> > When Chris caught you in tackle tag, he lowered you to the ground gently, so that you lay in his hard arms for a minute, looking up at him through that tangle of yellow hair, the green lawn wet below you. Sticks in your back. Blue eyes laughing at you. Wild knowledge in your heart.

We teach fragments as a way to distinguish between the complete sentence and the fragment and because fragments interjected into narrative can be effective. The fragments in this narrative create a more rapid pace and imply the fragmented observation and knowledge of preadolescence. They are deliberately inserted after a long, rhythmic sentence, to move the narrator and reader from a languorous pace to one more sudden and sharp. And they capture the jagged, throbbing intensity of physical passion's first stirrings.

Subject, Verb, and Object Forms

When we are using subjects and verbs, we need to look at subject-verb agreement. This is a simple notion; the subject and the verb should agree. Strunk and White put it nicely, saying: "The number of the subject determines the number of the verb" (2000, 9).

> Writers understand that if the subject is singular, so is the verb in the predicate. If the subject is plural, the verb in the predicate is plural too. That's why writers learn singular and plural forms of nouns, pronouns, and verbs.
>
> > Only one girl was caught that time.
> > All the girls were caught that time.

> Some pronouns that we'd expect to be plural are singular. These include *each*, *either*, *every*, *everyone*, *everybody*, *neither*, *nobody*, and *someone*.
>
> Every girl was caught that time.

The implications of this understanding are significant in terms of the knowledge it implies. Writers need to learn the singular and plural forms of subjects and verbs. This particularly means studying the pronouns and their forms and the irregular forms of verbs. It's somewhat easy to see the sense of how *he walks* changes to *we walk*; it's less easy to learn that *he is* changes to *we are*. We strive for repeated use in diverse situations and meaningful opportunities for students to employ these words in their own writing and speech. It's easier for students to remember these forms and how they agree if they hear proper usage in speech, and read it, and have opportunities to explore it in their own writing often. Memorization is tough. Trying to limit what students need to memorize is one reason we consider which forms of usage and terminology to teach young writers. Weaver puts it this way: "Teach to all students only those aspects of grammar that can help them write more effectively" (1996, 144).

Once we understand subject plus verb, their agreement, and their role in forming a sentence, it makes sense to consider *object*. Just as we considered the subject as both the subject of the sentence and the subject of the story, the object is the object of the story and the object of the sentence. We ask, therefore, Whom will Chris catch? Who else is in your story? Put someone in. That will be the object of the sentence, and here, the direct object of Chris's attention.

> Sometimes it is useful for writers to think about the idea of subject and object. In a sentence, the subject performs actions and the direct object receives action. The object is found in the sentence's predicate, as in this sentence, where *Chris* is the subject, *Lisa* the direct object, and *caught Lisa first* the predicate.
>
> Chris caught Lisa first.

The subject can also have an indirect object (whom or what this action gets passed on to after the direct object). In this sentence, *Chris* is the subject, the *push* is the direct object, and *Lisa* is the indirect object.

Chris gave Lisa a push.

Understanding subject and object helps us distinguish the proper forms of personal pronouns. Subject equals *I/you/he/she/we/they*. Object (direct or indirect) equals *me/you/him/her/us/them*.

I escaped Chris the first time, but just by a little.
Chris chased Lisa and me. I wanted her to just disappear.

Prepositions, such as *to, for, in, under, above, toward*, and *in between*, link subjects and verbs to objects. And if the object is a personal pronoun, we use its object form (*me, you, him, her, us*, or *them*).

Chris ran toward us.
Then Lisa ran in between Chris and me. She was a very fast runner.

It matters in English usage that we understand subject and object because the personal pronouns change form as they function as subject or object. Often student writers use too many undefined pronouns; sometimes it's hard to trace the movement of action around the characters because so many pronouns are used instead of names. The reader loses track and gets confused. So when we start using pronouns for subjects and objects, we realize how carefully we have to link our sentences so that the reader attaches the right meaning to our pronouns. We have to look at the words that came before the pronoun and see if we have given sufficient information to the reader. Is it Lisa who is caught?

There is also the tricky pronoun form that switches as it shifts function, the *who/whom*, which is another marker of higher literacy, whose correct usage moves us up in the hierarchy of language use. Amis despairs of its proper usage, saying that "except in funeral addresses and the like, or as a joke, *whom* is no longer heard from speakers of English" (1997, 242). Strunk and White, however, hold on to it, explaining that if it's the subject, whether in a sentence or in a clause, then it is *who*. If it is the object, it is *whom*.

> Understanding subject and object helps us know when to use *who* and when to use *whom.*
>
> Subject equals *who.*
> Whoever slowed down, even for a moment, was in danger.
>
> Object (direct or indirect or object of the preposition) equals *whom.*
> He could catch whomever he wanted.

Where are we, then, with the pronouns in the story? *I* escaped *him* the first time. Then *she* ran between *him* and *me. He* caught *her. I* wanted *her* to disappear. As we shift the function of the personal pronouns, we realize that writers need to know the proper forms of these pronouns. We also begin to see how pronouns act for the characters in the story: we see them moving around in the sentence the way they move around in the story, the way these characters move around on the wet, green lawn. It's *I* then it's *she* then it's *he* and *her*, then it's not *I* anymore, it's only *her.* A tangle of pronouns catching up to each other, leaving the narrator alone and bereft.

Verb Tense

Verbs not only indicate the relationship between subjects and objects in the sentence and story but also suggest how time shifts. Writers consider, therefore, the impact of verb tense on the tone of the story and on voice. Present tense gives a voice that differs from the tone of the same words put in past tense. One moves freely and dangerously in the world, the other moves with more knowledge and the wisdom gained from hindsight. We want to teach student writers to make effective choices about verb tense and then to maintain those choices by employing verb forms consistent with their choices.

Writers consider the tense in which they write, making choices about verb tense and maintaining verb forms consistent with those choices. Here are some ways writers consider verb tense:

Present tense often gives a sense of immediacy. It brings the reader into the story. It hints at a sense of things being unresolved. It can create tension, since the ending appears not yet experienced by the narrator. It implies a voice that is, in fact, writing from the age and events described in the piece. Present tense can be snappy and lively:

> We play every night from right after supper until it is dark and we hear our mothers calling, whistling, or ringing bells. Sometimes we play in our backyard, where there is a treehouse to hide in and a garage to run around.

Past tense often creates a voice that is marked by a sense of reflection, by a looking back on events in order to see and understand more, or in order to recover emotions or knowledge that has been buried. Past tense implies that the narrator has lived past these events and tells them now from an older vantage point. Past tense can be thoughtful and sometimes pensive. Past tense sometimes lets the narrator give foreshadowing from a position of greater knowledge than the character has in the story:

> When Chris caught you in tackle tag, he lowered you to the ground gently, so that you lay in his arms for a minute, looking up at him through that tangle of yellow hair, the green lawn wet below you.

Sometimes writers change tense in order to change the mood. A shift from past to present tense can evoke a sudden shift in perspective or voice, from one that is contemplative or distant to one that is more animated, sometimes more dangerous or provocative:

> Chris's hair was yellow, his eyes were blue, his bare arms and legs were brown. When his hard sixth-grade arms wrap around your fourth-grade body, holding you just off the ground, it is like nothing you ever knew before. It is something undomesticated.

A shift to future tense evokes still another perspective, one that shows time passing and a future that may be known, dreamt, or dreaded:

> Mrs. Terhaar's lawn will lose its muddy spots where we slipped. The grass will turn gold, and then brown, and then we will say how cold it's gotten. We'll put on our school clothes, cover our legs and arms, watch our skin grow pale again.

Verb tense is a lovely thing to consider and a wonderful subject for a class inquiry. Verb tense is related to point of view, to voice, to perspective. Writers who shift verb tense demonstrate their control of the story and their awareness of the reader—they move in and out of tenses deliberately in order to bring the reader closer to and farther away from action and from people. Sandra Cisneros does beautiful things with verb tense, sometimes shifting tense within a paragraph, and it is always worthwhile asking why. It is hopeless to ask students to memorize verb forms, particularly irregular verb endings, until they see the choice of verb tense as a meaningful one. We need to pay attention to tense in the stories we read and demonstrate how it is a meaningful choice in the stories we write. It's also worth playing around with verb tense. Sometimes writers put action in past tense and inner thinking in present. Sometimes they shift tenses to move from a big narrative to a smaller episode or event within it. It was the urge to demonstrate a shift in tense that shifted those hard sixth-grade arms to wrapping around a fourth-grade body in the present rather than in the past. That experimentation led to the illumination that present tense can keep that moment as one of infinite possibility—it's not contained in the past now, it sits here, now, always. We can locate those moments that have enduring possibility and mark them as present.

Punctuating Dialogue

When we consider story, we know that effective stories are often marked by a balance of action, inner thinking, and dialogue. And so we teach verbs and predicates, and we consider verb tense and perspective and voice, and we teach dialogue and how to punctuate it. We teach the formal punctuation of dialogue, although many modern writers have abandoned this form. And so we teach quotation marks, the use of commas, and the insertion of new paragraphs for dialogue.

> Writers who punctuate dialogue traditionally use quotation marks to indicate dialogue or direct speech. If the attribution—*he said* or *she said*—comes before the quoted speech, a comma is used after the *said*, and the dialogue terminates with

ending punctuation that is inside the quotation marks. If the attribution appears after the quoted speech, a comma replaces the end punctuation. In either case we start the dialogue with a capital letter. In dialogue, each speech is usually a new paragraph, even if it is one word. This helps the reader figure out who is speaking.

> The next time I let him catch me so that he would put his arms around me.
> He said, "You're not running very fast tonight."
> I said, "Really?"

Not all contemporary novelists follow this form anymore, but until one is a contemporary novelist, or sure of one's audience or purpose, it might be wise to.

Within dialogue, some writers abandon common usage in an effort to demonstrate the voice and education level of the speaker. This is a hard thing to do well. When we show our characters actually writing, as in when we include invented journals or letters in our piece, then perhaps we may include misusage that would be expected for that character. Sapphire does this to powerful effect in her novel *Push* (1997), as does Alice Walker in *The Color Purple* (1990). Most of the time, though, writers use proper usage to avoid a patronizing or artificial tone. Dialogue is useful for highlighting tension, for indicating the thinking of characters, for demonstrating action. When we move in dialogue down the page, jumping each line to a new speaker, with each speaker using the present tense, we introduce a new pace to the writing, a pace that is more like someone speaking than someone dreaming. It's a good contrast with the more contemplative, past-tense narration that came before it.

The Faithful Comma: Lists, Conjunctions, Longer Sentences

Clearly a woman who had issues with punctuation, Gertrude Stein calls the comma "servile" (1967, 131). Lynne Truss likewise gives it faint praise, saying that "using the comma well announces that you have an ear for sense and rhythm, confidence in your style and proper respect for your reader, but it does not mark you out as a master of your craft" (2003, 106). Perhaps the comma is servile in how utterly useful it is. Certainly it doesn't carry the mystery of the semicolon or the authority of the colon. But there is much to teach when we come to the comma. Commas help us tuck in lists and make these lists artful. Commas help us conjoin phrases and clauses so that we may write longer sentences. Commas are the Labrador retrievers of punctuation. Faithful, always at hand, sometimes underfoot.

The most visible use of the comma is the comma that separates items in a list.

Writers use commas to separate items in a list. The items can be nouns or actions.

Chris, David, Billy, Karen, Michael, Ben, Amy, Lisa, and me.
We heard our mothers calling, whistling, or ringing bells.

We can tuck items that go together in between the commas, and we can call attention to certain parts of the list by changing the order of the words:

Chris's hair was yellow, his eyes were blue, his bare arms and legs were brown.

The list can be a beautiful internal structure in sentences and in stories. Listing items joins them together, and it also separates out things that are different in the list. When we come upon Chris, his hair is yellow and his eyes are blue. But it is the bare brown skin on his arms and legs that gathers our attention because this part of the list is worded slightly differently.

One note about commas separating items in a list: writers find out what the house style is regarding that final comma that comes just before the last item. Some publishers, institutions, even nations, omit it. *Calling, whistling and ringing bells.* We teach students to find out what their teachers, professors, graders of tests and papers prefer, and we use this as a way to demonstrate that grammar is merely an agreed upon system that changes, sometimes slowly and sometimes rapidly, that coexists simultaneously with contradictory forms, that is constructed through various forces, among them the audience we're writing for.

After punctuating lists, what do commas do? They help us write longer, more varied sentences. It's a risky thing deciding to struggle with longer sentences, as long sentences can be ponderous, and they put us uncomfortably close to the rocky shores of mispunctuation. We cut them up instead. We tend to shorten them. Short sentences can be snappy. They can also be annoying. As Theodore Geisel (Dr. Seuss) puts it, "simple, short sentences don't always work. You have to do tricks with pacing, alternate long sentences with short, to keep it vital and alive" (in Murray 1990, 160). And so we study usage in order to compose more complex sentences.

The comma is used to join two complete sentences in the following ways. We have one complete sentence, and we can join it to another with a conjunction and a comma. On the other hand, when we join a complete sentence with an *incomplete* sentence, we do *not* use a comma. We have one complete sentence and one incomplete clause that usually lacks a subject. We can make most decisions this way; however, some conjunctions are more demanding. Joining sentences with *however* or *nevertheless* demands something more noticeable than the comma; that is, the semicolon. The stickler will notice here that the preceding sentences demonstrate their points. To make these rules comprehensible and viable to nongrammar fanatics, we have to write some examples and study their impact on the story.

> When we join two complete sentences (both having a subject and a predicate) using the conjunctions *and, but, or, yet, so,* and *nor,* we use a comma.
>
> Lisa had brown hair and slim legs. She was a very fast runner.
> Lisa had brown hair and slim legs, and she was a very fast runner.
>
> When we join a complete sentence (subject, predicate) with an incomplete sentence or clause (usually lacking a subject) using these conjunctions (*and, but, yet, so, nor*), we do *not* use a comma. Usually there's only one subject, so we don't want to separate that subject from the rest of the sentence.
>
> Lisa had brown hair and slim legs and was a very fast runner.

We see that we have choices in how we join our sentences, and that if we want a more rapid pace, we may choose the form that allows us to omit the comma. If we want a slower, more deliberate pace, we choose the form that asks the reader to pause at the comma. Lisa is moving fast in our narrative, so we choose the form that does not have any commas. *Lisa had brown hair and slim legs and was a very fast runner.* We add our longer sentences to our narrative, putting them in where we feel they accomplish the most, and the story begins to have more flair. That's what usage can do for us.

Now we come to the usage that allows us to write yet more complicated sentences with and without commas. This is where our heads begin to pound as we leaf through the style and usage manuals, desperately trying to come to terms with nominals, participial phrases, subordinate clauses, appositives, unmovable modifiers, correlative conjunctions, absolutes, adverbial prepositional phrases, restrictive clauses, predicate nominatives, and more. Here is what we encounter in our research: "One frequent kind of free modifier is the adverbial, including the adverb clause . . . the other kind is the adjectival, including appositives, participial phrases, and adjective clauses that are set off by commas (but the adjective clauses are not movable, unlike most free modifiers)" (Weaver 1996, 250). We want to understand, but we feel as if we are going mad. And if we feel our patience and our comprehension straining, we can only imagine what our students must feel when faced with such an arcane and complicated system.

But then we remember that if we ever did know what an unmovable modifier was, we don't anymore, and we write anyway. We write in longer sentences, we make punctuation decisions as we write, and our usage is proper most of the time. So what are we doing? We simply strive for clarity, putting in punctuation so that it enhances meaning. If we really get stuck, we either check a reference manual or recast our sentence. Mostly, we use forms we have seen before. Sometimes we return to the rules we already know and assume they still apply as our sentences get longer.

We avoid terms like *appositives, participial phrases,* and so on. Strunk and White don't use any of these terms. Indeed, Strunk originally limited the really important usage rules to five. Here are some ways to punctuate more complicated sentences, and descriptions of the usage rules that govern this punctuation, as we understand and use them.

> Writers sometimes attach more description to the subject or predicate; if you can imagine this description in parentheses, then you enclose it with commas. (These additions are called *parenthetic expressions.*) Follow your instincts or learn the complicated rules for clauses.

Chris (who was the fastest runner on our block) caught everyone when we played tag.

Chris, who was the fastest runner on our block, caught everyone when we played tag.

If the description is critical to the meaning of the sentence, then we don't enclose it in commas, so the reader understands that this description is no light matter. If the sentence below had commas around *in tackle tag*, the reader would wonder if the players were playing other tag games and if these other games also involved the players being knocked to the ground:

The tag in tackle tag consisted of being knocked to the ground.

Many of our punctuation choices are not, however, based on usage; they are based on the urge to make our meaning specific. As John Dawkins says, "anyone—writer or student—will punctuate more effectively and efficiently because of a concern for meaning rather than a concern for rules" (in Noden 1999, 96). A comma can arrange and align items, a comma can separate out and it can bring together. Here's how it looks:

Sometimes how we use commas indicates a slightly different meaning, as below. In the first sentence, only some girls experience Chris's arms in tackle tag.

The girls who were often caught by Chris glimpsed a hint of untamed experience.

In this sentence, all the girls get caught equally:

The girls, who were often caught by Chris, glimpsed a hint of untamed experience.

Now the boys can be caught, first some, and then all:

The boys who were also caught by Chris must have felt something too.

Surely, the boys who were also caught by Chris must have felt something too.

The boys, who were also caught by Chris, must have felt something too.

Our commas acknowledge desires, within and across gender; they know that love follows few rules. We add these sentences to the narrative, inserting them where we feel they will do the most good. In the next lesson we show our commas becoming flirtatious.

Sometimes the use of commas is suggestive. This first example suggests that there is time for the narrator to take a breath between being caught and feeling those arms.

> The next time I let him catch me, so that he would wrap his arms around me.

Everything happens very fast in the next example.

> The next time I let him catch me so that he would wrap his arms around me.

We could slow it down even more, flirting, as it were, by putting in two commas:

> The next time, I let him catch me, so that he would wrap his arms around me.

Sometimes punctuation has more to do with style than anything else. It is style, as it exists as a tool for the writer, but it becomes voice in a piece when it is deliberate and effective. We see voice in some sentences where commas suggest time passing slowly or swiftly for the narrator. We see voice in the deliberate use of commas and the deliberate lack of them. We see voice in how commas bring characters and emotions together and how they separate them. We see voice in how commas mark space within the sentence, how they suggest beginnings and endings and also middles. Thurber, in *The Years with Ross*, gives this anecdote about a comma inserted in his prose by *New Yorker* editor Harold Ross:

> A professor of English somewhere in England wrote me ten years ago . . . he picked out this sentence in a *New Yorker* casual of mine: "After dinner, the men went into the living room," and he wanted to know why I, or the editors, had put in the comma. I could explain that one all right. I wrote back that this particular comma was Ross's way of giving the men time to push back their chairs and stand up. (2001, 236)

Surely, Thurber's explanation of the comma after dinner is, as Truss calls it, "one of the loveliest things ever said about punctuation" (2003, 70). In the story we're writing, we'll keep the second example, the one where it happens very fast, because in this story the narrator just lost her chance to feel Chris's arms because another girl was faster. This time there will be a more rapid pace. No commas, and its own paragraph. No room for others no time for the men to push back their chairs no time for other girls to intervene.

The Apostrophe

When we dare to put our commas to work in risky ways, we know we have an intimate relationship with punctuation. We have the courage to turn, then, to look more closely at something that haunts grammarians: the apostrophe. We have waited until now for the apostrophe because while it is certainly bothersome when it is used incorrectly, it rarely denudes a piece of meaning and there were other things to get to first. Beginning and ending punctuation, commas, paragraphs—these add more power to writing. The apostrophe is more a marker of conventional literacy; it is like *who/whom* in how it exposes the blunderer. Unlike the comma, whose appearance creates meaning and tone, apostrophes are hardly noticeable when used correctly. As Truss puts it, "using the apostrophe correctly is a mere negative proof: it tells the world you are not a thicko" (2003, 105).

Amis says darkly that "the rules governing the use of this vexing little mark are evidently hard to master," a statement, we admit, that does not instill confidence (1997, 14). Nevertheless, we forge ahead, if only because the apostrophe is used to show possession, and that is a meaningful reason to master the apostrophe. Like many narratives, this is a story where some long for possession, so the apostrophe must appear. So we show students some ways it is used.

> Apostrophes are used to show possession. To show possession, we follow these rules:
>
> It comes before the *s* with a singular noun, and after the *s* with a plural noun. Names ending in *s* still add an *'s* except for Jesus or those from antiquity.

> Indefinite pronouns (*one, somebody, somebody else*) add *'s*, with the exception of *who* and *it*, which become *whose* and *its*.
>
> An apostrophe is *not* used with personal pronouns (*mine, his, her, hers, your, yours, our, ours, their, theirs*).
>
> Chris's blue gaze, his brown hands, set many girls' hearts beating.
>
> Some boys' hearts, undoubtedly, beat also for Chris, and his for theirs.
>
> Jesus' disciples maybe felt like we did for Chris.
>
> When he looked down at you, your heart's rhythm changed and the blood altered course in your veins.
>
> He was like a young god, with his beauty that was like Achilles'.
>
> Tackle tag often felt like the Trojan War, with all its jealousies and betrayals.
>
> An apostrophe also marks time (perhaps thought of as possession of time). In two week's time summer would end, and so would tackle tag on Mrs. Terhaar's lawn.

We push ourselves to use an abundance of apostrophes and possessive forms, and we push our narrative into unexpected places. Hearts begin to beat a little faster. Our narrative use of these forms, of course, reflects urges beyond the grammatical. Like our commas, ours are antihomophobic apostrophes. They take possession of the heart regardless of gender. Grammar is interesting this way, in how we harness it in suggestive ways. Eve Sedgwick talks about the closet of grammar, the way certain forms such as the passive tense, and the subjunctive, were used in nineteenth-century literature to contain and disguise notions considered unpleasant, such as the homosexual (1990, 119). Our use of grammar in the story attempts the opposite: it attempts to unfetter desire. Our apostrophes liberate girls' and boys' hearts on this summer evening. Readers may make other choices, but it's interesting to make these choices, to see how grammar can be redolent with desires and how the unsafe stories we tell emerge through grammatical choices. We include and comment on this here as a way to demonstrate that all teaching is tangled up with our notions of how the world should be.

So take up issues, if you wish, as you take up apostrophes. E. B. White tells us to love the way that "all writers, by the way they use the language, reveal something of their spirits, their habits, their capacities, and their biases" (Strunk and White 2000, 67). Especially when our instruction places such emphasis on rules, we like the narrative to be one that hints of pleasure and transgression. The writing and the identities it suggests remain open to possibility even as we embrace more usage, including other ways to use the apostrophe.

An apostrophe signifies contractions or missing letters. An apostrophe always marks the contraction of *it is* or *it has* to *it's*. (*Its* refers to possession.)

Mrs. Terhaar's lawn will lose its muddy spots where we slipped.

The grass will turn gold, and then brown, and then we will say how cold it's gotten.

Common contractions substitute an apostrophe for some of the letters in the following verbs: *is, are, will, would, not.* The apostrophe takes the place of all the letters except the last one or two in the substituted word. *We would* becomes *we'd. We will* becomes *we'll. We are* becomes *we're.*

We'll put on our school clothes, cover our legs and arms, watch our skin grow pale again. At the elementary school, girls and boys have gym separately. Boys can't tackle girls and lower them gently to the ground. A girl in fourth grade and a boy in sixth grade won't glimpse each other slowing down.

An apostrophe always marks the contraction of *who is* or *who has* to *who's*.

We won't hear any more those words, "Whose lawn should we use tonight?"
Or, "Who's 'it'?"
Or, "Chris is."

The proper use of apostrophes is indeed deemed a marker of literacy. One senses Truss's hostility when she says: "If the word does not stand for 'it is' or 'it has' then what you require is 'its.' *This is extremely easy to grasp*" (2003, 43). No exclamation point, but the italics are expressive. We don't dare check what Fowler has to say about this misusage, fearful of being belittled even more.

The Semicolon and the Colon

The semicolon and the colon bring a grin to the face of a writer who has studied usage. Few understand them, fewer still use them artfully, which means that the writer who feels confident wielding semicolons and colons feels particularly powerful. The most common usage for semicolons is to join two sentences using *however* or *nevertheless*.

> When we join two sentences using *however* or *nevertheless*, we use a semicolon rather than a comma.
>
> Lisa had been my best friend since kindergarten; nevertheless, I wanted her to disappear. I wanted the ground to open up and swallow her shiny hair and her white teeth and her long fast legs; however, that's not what happened.

Like knowing the difference between *who* and *whom*, knowing that *however* is preceded by a semicolon is part of the language of power. There is more to the semicolon, though. The semicolon is artful. We love the semicolon because it is provocative. Here are some things the semicolon can do:

> The semicolon can create a feeling of suspense; there is more to know than what is stated in the first part.
>
> Chris admired kids who were fast; you could never just let him catch you. Whoever slowed down, even for a moment, was in danger; he could catch whomever he wanted.
>
> The semicolon creates intimacy between two sentences that could stand on their own. It implies that one sentence is related closely to the other.
>
> Chris's hand was on her back; she stumbled and began to fall.

The semicolon suggests relationships; it implies knowledge without making it explicit. We wonder if Chris's touch causes Lisa to stumble, or if she stumbles in order to feel his touch. Lisa's behavior was often ambiguous, and her motivations were complicated. The semicolon introduces ambiguity; it implies complexity, sometimes even complicity.

The colon, on the other hand, is more definitive than the semicolon. It has authority. The colon puts hair on our chest and verve in our writing. Composing with colons is like drinking single-malt Scotch. Here are some ways colons are used:

The colon introduces lists, particularly lists with large items, which we separate by semicolons.

This is what coursed through your blood when you felt Chris behind you: terror that you would be caught; dread that you would escape; and impatience to feel more.

The colon indicates clear causality.

Chris's hand was on her back: she stumbled and began to fall.

The colon makes things that were doubtful or only suggested, lucid. Where the semicolon implied that Lisa perhaps stumbles in order to be caught, the colon says that she fell only after being caught. The semicolon is a marker of intimacy and it implies a close relationship. The colon is a marker of time passing, and thus it implies consequence. With the colon, we say, "Ah-ha. She stumbled because he knocked her." We, however, remain suspicious and will retain the semicolon in the narrative.

Colons and semicolons push us to think hard about action, about perspective, about relationships. They are punctuation that asks us to decide when to be explicit and when to be subtle. They are also punctuation that defines their audience. They assume a close reader. Semicolons and colons express confidence in both the writer and the reader.

There are a couple of other interesting ways to use the colon.

The colon introduces a significant question or statement.

When you felt Chris's arms around you, holding you just off the ground, you wondered: what would it feel like if this weren't tag?

When we use a colon to introduce a question like this, it is a window into the inner thinking of a character. The colon launches us, without the interruption of quotation marks or the blatant speaking voice of dialogue. The colon here guards the door into the heart of the narrator. The colon can also do this by putting two things together and showing where the narrator stands on these issues.

> The colon puts two statements together that define each other—the second one either explains the first or clearly denies it.
>
> This I knew for sure: I would never miss a game of tackle tag if Chris were playing.
>
> It was tag: it was something else entirely.

The Dash

There is one more punctuation mark that connects clauses, phrases, and some times sentences—the dash. Like the apostrophe, the dash and its misuse have outraged grammarians. Open Fowler and Fowler to the heading "Dashes," and you'll find these words: "These are the realms of chaos" ([1906] 2002, 262). Fowler and Fowler continue with ten pages of small print in which they denounce common misuses of the dash. We, however, are not so dismissive; we love the dash for the way it creates rhythms and can complicate thought and sentences, though we understand that it can be abused. It is a familiar form in email texts, for instance, where it seems to replace all other punctuation. (Hey Sally—let's go to Sarah's party tonight—Madonna will be there—Really!) This use of the dash is akin to the use of the exclamation point, and so we teach students to use it sparingly, so it doesn't become a stylistic tic. And we teach it, too, to clarify the difference between the dash and the hyphen.

> The dash connects phrases and sentences. A dash is twice the length of the hyphen.
>
> Tackle tag—these words still conjure magic.

> The hyphen connects words. The hyphen is half the length of the dash.
>
> I was a ten-year-old in the summer of fourth grade, and I would not feel a boy's arms around me like that again until I was seventeen.

Of the hyphen, Fowler and Fowler say: "hyphens are regrettable necessities, and to be done without when they reasonably may" ([1906] 2002, 271). Six pages of small print follow, but this statement sums it up. We teach their use for numbers and ages. Seven-year-old. Twenty-one. Some writers do more interesting things with hyphens, connecting words to suggest identity. Hyphen-wielding-usage-master-gate-breaker-grammar-maven.

Split Infinitives and Other Dangerous Liaisons

The previous are the rules of usage that we find most inform our writing practices. Intimacy with these rules extends our powers. Using them to compose gives us fluency in our writing and our teaching. We offer what we consider the most important usage rules, but of course there are others. The realization that other usage rules exist and remain unstudied can stymie us. Sometimes we prohibit any usage that makes us uneasy. We're not sure that *to boldly go* is actually wrong, but we worry that it is, or we fear that it offends some, and so we forbid it. No split infinitives for our students. This is a dangerous practice, as it can lead us to become more than sticklers—it can lead to pettiness and the refusal of our students to take risks in their writing. Moreover, sometimes usage is more permissive than we thought. The following notes, gathered from Kingsley Amis's *The King's English: A Guide to Modern Usage* (1997), clarify some common grammatical misunderstandings:

> There is a misplaced notion that sentences must not begin or end with a preposition. Amis calls this idea "one of those fancied prohibitions (compare split infinitives) dear to ignorant snobs" (166).
>
> To us he was like a god.

That seems to put this notion to bed. *To be or not to be* has survived the test of time, and we may permit student writers this usage as it is permitted by the defender of the King's English. More significantly, the urge to avoid starting or ending sentences with prepositions alters voice and meaning. As we try to re-cast *For me, he was the only creature on earth who really mattered,* we can do it by moving the *for me* to the end, but it changes the tone of the sentence; it takes away that sense of self-absorbency that marks this as a preadolescent voice, and it makes what *mattered* matter less by removing the word from its key position and burying it deeper in the sentence. The original sentence shows that everything for this narrator is always first and foremost *for me.*

Now for the misconception that we cannot begin a sentence with *and* or *but*:

> Amis says, "The idea that *and* must not begin a sentence, or even a paragraph, is an empty superstition. The same goes for *but*. Indeed either word can give unimprovably early warning of the sort of thing that is to follow" (14).
>
> To us he was like a god, with his beauty that was like Achilles'. And tackle tag often felt like the Trojan War, with all its jealousies and betrayals.

The use of *and* to start a sentence often gives a natural voice to student writing and a lovely liquid flow. *But* tells the reader that the writer has ideas, and there is complexity in the writing, and we should pay attention. Things are not simple as we may at first think when *but* begins a sentence.

And so, on to the split infinitive.

> The rule against split infinitives, is, to quote Amis again, "the best known of the imaginary rules that petty linguistic tyrants seek to lay upon the English language. There is no grammatical reason whatever against splitting an infinitive and often the avoidance of one lands the writer in trouble" (218).
>
> A girl in fourth grade and a boy in sixth grade won't glimpse each other slowing down, waiting to be tenderly caught on a wet green lawn.

Split infinitives are permissible, although they are easy to recast if your audience includes those whom split infinitives offend. If the recasting doesn't change meaning, then it is easy to please all. Sometimes, though, recasting changes meaning. We like that the tenderness comes in the middle of the catch—it is a deliberate construction, *to be tenderly caught*. We could wait for the tenderness too, having it come after the catch, recasting it as *to be caught tenderly*. What matters is that we can consider this choice and how moving words in a sentence affects the rhythm and meaning. Moving the adverb makes us wait longer; it brings the harsher sound of *catch* before the more mellifluous, loving sound of *tenderly*.

Rhythm matters. It is when we pay attention to the rhythm of words that we know we love language. It is concern with rhythm that leads us to write longer and shorter sentences, sentences with many clauses, followed sometimes by fragments. Amis does not take up the issue of fragments. Weaver, however, does, and she says that they are allowable when used judiciously and for deliberate effect (1996, 249). Strunk and White agree.

And so we find that we may, indeed, start sentences with *and* or *but*, that we may boldly or tenderly split infinitives, that we may use fragments at will. We may, however, want to caution students about the need to consider one's audience before embracing these forms. As Amis puts it, "anti-split infinitive fanatics are beyond reason" (1997, 218). The intent of our choices will be lost on those who stand ready to be offended. Also, as Amis warns, "people with strong erroneous views about 'correct' English are just the sort of people who consider your application for a job, decide whether you are 'educated' or not, wonder about your general suitability for this and that" (218). We must be daring, but we must dare wisely.

We offer these clarifications because we prefer to teach students what writers can do, rather than what they cannot or should not. We believe that if student writers strive for clarity, they will mostly do well. But they also should be allowed to make attempts that do not achieve what was hoped for, but that show courage.

The Story

When we look at the completed narrative, we see the effect of usage in the variety of our sentence structure and the diverse meanings achieved by punctuation. We find, also, that exploring usage led us to explore new territory as writers.

Colons no longer daunt us. We develop a way with semicolons. We shift tenses in order to move our reader to different places. Our way with grammar is part of our voice, part of our power, part of our art. Here is the story:

Tackle Tag

In summer all the kids on our block played tackle tag. Chris, David, Billy, Karen, Michael, Ben, Amy, Lisa, and me. We played every night from right after supper until it was dark and we heard our mothers calling, whistling, or ringing bells. Sometimes we played in our backyard, where there was a treehouse to hide in and a garage to run around. But mostly we played on Mrs. Terhaar's lawn, where there was no place to get away, and the sidewalk, the street corner, and the driveway edged us in.

It made a difference if you were fast. It made a difference to Chris. Chris admired kids who were fast; you could never just let him catch you. Chris was the fastest runner, and the most beautiful too. Chris was often "it." Chris's hair was yellow, his eyes were blue, his bare arms and legs were brown. The tag in tackle tag consisted of being knocked to the ground. When his hard sixth-grade arms wrap around your fourth-grade body, holding you just off the ground, it is like nothing you ever knew before. It is something undomesticated.

Chris, who when he was twelve was the fastest runner and truly heartbreakingly beautiful, caught everyone when we played tackle tag. Whoever slowed down, even for a moment, was in danger; he could catch whomever he wanted. This is what coursed through your blood when you felt Chris behind you: terror that you would be caught; dread that you would escape; and impatience to feel more. When you felt Chris's arms around you, holding you just off the ground, you wondered: what would it feel like if this weren't tag? I escaped Chris the first time, but only by a little. Then Lisa ran in between Chris and me. Lisa had brown hair and slim legs and was a very fast runner. Chris caught Lisa first. Lisa had been my best friend since kindergarten; nevertheless, I wanted her to disappear. Chris's hand was on her back; she stumbled and began to fall. Only one girl was caught that time.

The next time I let him catch me so that he would put his arms around me.

He said, "You're not running very fast tonight."

I said, "Really?"

Chris's blue gaze and strong arms set many girls' hearts beating. The girls who were often caught by Chris glimpsed a hint of untamed experience. Surely, the boys who were also caught by Chris must have felt something too.

Some boys' hearts, undoubtedly, beat also for Chris, and his for theirs. Jesus' disciples maybe felt like we did for Chris. When he looked down at you your heart's rhythm changed and the blood altered course in your veins. To us he was like a god, with his beauty that was like Achilles'. And tackle tag often felt like the Trojan War, with all its jealousies and betrayals. This I knew for sure: I would never miss a game of tackle tag if Chris were playing.

In two week's time summer would end, and so would tackle tag on Mrs. Terhaar's lawn. Mrs. Terhaar's lawn will lose its muddy spots where we slipped. The grass will turn gold, and then brown, and then we will say how cold it's gotten. We'll put on our school clothes, cover our legs and arms, watch our skin grow pale again. At the elementary school, girls and boys have gym separately. Boys can't tackle girls and lower them gently to the ground. A girl in fourth grade and a boy in sixth grade won't glimpse each other slowing down, waiting to be tenderly caught on a wet green lawn. We won't hear any more those words, "Whose lawn should we use tonight?"

Or, "Who's 'it'?"

Or, "Chris is."

Tackle tag—these words still conjure magic. I was ten years old in the summer of fourth grade, and I would not feel a boy's arms around me again like that until I was seventeen. It was tag: it was something else entirely. When Chris caught you in tackle tag, he lowered you to the ground gently, so that you lay in his arms for a minute, looking up at him through that tangle of yellow hair, the green lawn wet below you. Sticks in your back. Blue eyes laughing at you. Wild knowledge in your heart.

Love and Sedition

Getting Intimate with Grammar by
Breaking the Rules

You must break all the rules of painting, but you must also convince me
you've had a reason to do so.

— HANS HOFFMAN, ARTIST

I n the previous chapter we discussed how we, as teachers, must strive to
empower students to engage with the world and realize their full poten
tial by arming them with the knowledge and skills that our society has established as norms. To do otherwise is to shirk our duty and risk sending our
students out in the world unprepared and ill equipped. Avoiding the teaching
of grammar and conventions is, thus, an act of neglect that, whether we consciously intend it or not, abets a system of marginalization that denies some
students the opportunities of full participation in the world—or, as American
Express so elitistly puts it, the benefits of membership.

We are committed, then, to take on the difficult work of teaching grammar
and to find ways of talking and thinking about it that makes our students want
to take it on, too, if only to fight the forces of marginalization. But students will
need more than by-the-book grammar to succeed in the world. They will need
to be innovators and creative thinkers, problem solvers and pioneers, or else
they risk being marginalized again, condemned to the ranks of the functional.
Recently we attended a staff development day where our Australian colleagues
pointed to a study conducted by the state of Victoria that asked the executives of
successful Australian firms what they looked for in an upper-level employee.

Rather than listing traits like organization, punctuality, and good verbal skills, they said they wanted people who could think outside the box, who had the capacity for original thought and a mind for innovation.

Of course, one might argue that they wanted employees who had that and good verbal skills, too, for what is the point of original thought if it cannot be expressed succinctly and clearly so that it is understood? We concede the point fully and have no intention of shying away from our commitment. But to provide the latter without the former—to teach the skills without teaching thinking—leaves our students disenfranchised again, shut out from the range of opportunities that more original thinkers can access. And it confuses the means with the end: We need to provide students with grammatical knowledge so that their voices can be heard, not so that they can fit into a system of uniformity. They need to own the rules of grammar, not be enslaved to them, so that they can manipulate and use them, each to their own unique end. In *Imagination in Teaching and Learning,* Kieran Egan describes this friction when he says: "There is, of course, a constant tension in education between teaching the conventions whereby students will have to live and encouraging the capacities that enable them to gain some kind of mental freedom from those conventions" (1992, 48).

But how do we teach in a way that values rules and innovative thinking at once, which we want to do so that our instruction doesn't seem compartmentalized—and so that we don't seem hypocritical, applying one set of expectations to one subject and a vastly different set to another? How do we make our instruction of grammar be about more than conformity while still promoting adherence? And how do we teach it in lasting ways that additionally address our other desire to give students a feel for the beauty of language, for its power and strength and grace, so that they want to write, and write well, in a satisfying, pleasurable way? Or put another way, how do we provide students with aesthetic experiences in addition to practical ones, so that they can experience all the wonders the world gives us at both personal and public levels?

To disentangle this conundrum, we turn to writers, knowing that they have the utmost respect and admiration for language, for the beauty of words and the power of syntax and the potent subtleties of punctuation—and knowing, as well, that they often veer from textbook standards of usage. And what we find is that they have a different relationship with grammar than most students do, one that is, indeed, marked by pleasure and satisfaction, not boredom, frustration, and dread. We read Pico Iyer, who talks about "punctuation as a labor of love" (1996, 82), and Donald Murray, who likens wordplay to a tryst with an old, delightful lover. We reacquaint ourselves with the Russian writer Babel, who says that "no iron can pierce the heart with such force as a period put in just the right place," and we take on trust Barbara Tuchman's claim that "nothing is more satisfying than to write a good sentence" (in Murray 1990, 137).

Again and again writers attest to the satisfaction that is there to be had by fully engaging with language, by twisting and tinkering and twirling it around in a way that our students rarely have. But how do we help our students develop this kind of relationship, since we know that most find the study of grammar something that's far less than pleasurable, and have never been known, to our ears at least, to equate it with matters as urgent and lofty and emotional as pierced hearts and love?

To get students engaged in grammar this way, we need to make it seductive, something they can't resist. We need to make them want to play with it, to dig in and get their hands dirty. We need to stop imposing it on them and invite them to explore it with us, discovering for themselves why the rules are there and what meaningful purpose they serve. And so with caution and a bit of trepidation, we opened the door to experimentation, to breaking the rules in a way that provides a better understanding of their actual function, which in turn leads to respect at the same time it promotes the kind of creative thinking that leads to innovation and art. Go ahead, we say, as Hans Hoffman did, break the rules if you see fit, but you need to tell me the purpose it served—a requirement that acknowledges that students know the rules and what's gained and lost by discarding them.

What follows, then, are our experiments and experiences with rule breaking. We begin by conducting an inquiry into a text that breaks all the rules to powerful ends and effects, then take a look at how one student discovers his voice as a writer by apprenticing himself to it. Then we share the story of a class that embarked on a study of grammar and voice, starting by looking at how the unit was planned and then recounting how it played it out, with additional thoughts on classroom practice and how to read like a writer along the way.

A Radical Inquiry: A First Look at the Text

We begin by looking at one of the most radical, rule-breaking texts we could find: "justice," by w. r. rodriguez (1998), a piece that departs so much from the norm, it defies the standard categories of genre. We reprint it here in the exact way it appears in *Welcome to Your Life*, an almost square block of unpunctuated text without any capital letters:

justice

a youth grabbed an old woman's purse fat with tissues and aspirin and such sundries as old women carry in sagging purses a desperate youth nice enough not to beat her head bloody into the sidewalk as muggers of the feeble often do for the fun of it i suppose and he ran up the hill but one of the perennial watchers watched it all from her window the purseless old woman in slow pursuit yelling such curses as it takes old women a lifetime to learn but it was too danger-ous too futile the silent watcher knew to call the police who might come and rough up someone they did not like just for the fun of it i suppose or who would talk polite and feel mad inside and roll their eyes because there was really nothing they could do and there were murders and assaults to handle so this silent angry watcher carelessly but carefully dropped flower pots from her fourth floor windowsill garden one crashing before one behind and the third hitting him on the head a geranium i suppose and closed her window while the huffing grateful old woman looked up at the heavens to thank the lord and walked off with her purse laughing when she finally calmed down and leaving the youth to awaken in the blue arms of the law and do you know two smiling cops walked up all those stairs to warn the watcher that if she weren't more careful with her plants she would get a ticket for littering i suppose (1998, 78)

If we notice what there is to be noticed, we will see what we described earlier: a block of words that at first glance seems dense and almost impenetrable, in good part because there is not a punctuation mark in sight. If we attend to how we react to this, we may feel puzzlement or frustration, perhaps even be put off or skeptical. How are we expected to make our way through this without the signposts of conventions? Are we being toyed with by some smart-aleck writer who is playing some kind of game?

We ask students this: to notice what there is to be noticed and to try to articulate their reaction to it. Almost always students are intrigued, having never seen anything quite like it before. But as we first were, they are often at a loss about just how to proceed. We can ask students then to think about what strategies they may have learned to help us here, to engage them in a conversation about possible plans of attack. Or we may simply reveal straightaway what strategy we used: to read the piece so it was comprehensible and not just a string of random words, we needed to punctuate it in our heads, to mentally provide the stop signs of periods and the commas that signal a pause.

We read the piece aloud then, imbuing it with all the drama and meaning we can—meaning that we were able to construct by mentally punctuating. Inevitably, students think that it's "cool," in terms of both content and form. But before we go on to discuss the content, we show our students what we did in our heads by either asking them to punctuate it or placing the following punctuated version of the text on an overhead:

Justice

A youth grabbed an old woman's purse, fat with tissues and aspirin and such sundries as old women carry in sagging purses—a desperate youth, nice enough not to beat her head bloody into the sidewalk as muggers of the feeble often do (for the fun of it, I suppose). And he ran up the hill, but one of the perennial watchers watched it all from her window: the purseless old woman in slow pursuit yelling such curses as it takes old women a lifetime to learn. But it was too dangerous, too futile; the silent watcher knew to call the police, who might come and rough up someone they did not like (just for the fun of it, I suppose), or who would talk polite and feel mad inside and roll their eyes because there was really nothing they could do, and there were murders and assaults to handle. So this silent, angry watcher carelessly, but carefully, dropped flower pots from her fourth-floor windowsill garden, one crashing before, one behind, and the third hitting him on the head (a geranium, I suppose) and closed her window while the huffing, grateful old woman looked up at the heavens to thank the lord and walked off with her purse, laughing when she finally calmed down and leaving the youth to awaken in the blue arms of the law. And do you know? Two smiling cops walked up all those stairs to warn the watcher that if she weren't more careful with her plants she would get a ticket (for littering, I suppose).

This drives home one critical teaching point: that punctuation actually helps us make meaning and sense of texts. It is not just a system of symbols and rules designed to give students headaches, but an actual navigational tool to help us make our way through a maze of words that we might otherwise get lost in. And we draw the students' attention to how much punctuation we used in order to make the piece readable: not just commas and periods, but parentheses, a question mark, dashes. We also note that this is how *we* did it—this is how we *chose* to do it—knowing there were other options. One could set off the phrases we placed in parentheses, for instance, with dashes instead, replace the semicolon with a period, omit or add a comma. We did it this way because this way supports how we interpreted the piece. We set the narrator's interjections in parentheses, for example, rather than using dashes, because we imagine him off to the side, standing apart from the action he's witnessed with his suppositions and comments, and parentheses seemed to capture that more—seemed to isolate him more—than we thought dashes would. And we employed a semicolon where we did (*But it was too dangerous, too futile; the silent watcher knew to call the police*) because we thought it was the silent watcher who thought it was dangerous and futile, and because of that she did what she did. The semicolon, we thought, would suggest that causality and connection more than a period would, though a period would probably be more apt if you thought that it was the narrator or the purseless old woman who felt that the chase was too dangerous and futile.

Extending the Inquiry: Reading Like a Writer

Depending on a variety of factors—how much time we have, where we are in the school year, how skilled our students are becoming with this work, how comfortable we feel with it ourselves—we might distribute copies of the original text to the class and ask the students, in pairs, to punctuate it according to how they've interpreted it, keeping in mind the way that punctuation helps establish both meaning and connections. Whether we take this route or not, though, we want to draw the class's attention to another teaching point: that punctuation is both a navigational tool and an interpretative, artistic one. It helps us, as readers, make our way through texts, signaling when to pause and stop, alerting us to switches in action and thought. And it helps us, as writers, more clearly convey what it is we want our readers to feel by subtly reinforcing characterization, making connections, creating tone.

This understanding is critical if we're to change our students' relationship to grammar, which will deepen even more as we address the next question: Why did the author choose to write the piece this way, without those navigational and interpretative guides? Was he trying just to be faddish or clever or novel for novelty's sake? Is it just some kind of habit or tic, carried over from the way he writes his name, in all lowercase letters? Or is there something else going on here, something that will add to both our understanding and enjoyment of the piece if we inquire further?

So we pose some questions: We have seen how helpful punctuation can be in understanding this piece, so why might have the author gotten rid of all of it? What is gained by leaving out the punctuation? What effects are achieved? We can ask students to consider these questions with a partner, sharing their thoughts, which we would chart, with the whole class after several minutes. Or we could ask them to take a few minutes to stop and jot their thoughts in a notebook, again sharing out loud so that the whole class could benefit from individual student thinking. And if the questions spark much thought and controversy, we can even use the structure of accountable talk to let the students bat their thoughts around, posit their ideas and test them out on their peers.

At some point, we need to share our own thoughts with our students, modeling for them how to make connections between *how* a piece is written and *what* it is about or, put another way, how a writer's choices, even at the level of punctuation and grammar, can inform and support the content. And we do this by talking about how the piece and the grammatical choices affect us. If they haven't already said so, we will tell our students that the way the piece begins, with no paragraph indentation and no capital letter, makes us feel that what is recounted here is just a snippet of some larger whole, a slice of life from an urban day that is filled with similar incidents, equally random and chaotic. Who knows what the narrator might witness next as he continues down the street. We sense the possibility that it might be as quirky and surprising as what he's seen here from the fact that there is no true ending to the piece; there's no period to tell us it is over. And there's a sense that events are spinning out of control, that things are happening fast. The mugging, the chase, the flower pots crashing: it all comes at us in one unstoppable rush, which again is reinforced by the fact that we have no punctuation marks to help us catch our breath.

But we do pause a moment to ponder the title—"justice," in lowercase letters. And we decide that that somehow feels right. This is, after all, not about official justice, with a capital *J*. This has nothing to do with juries and courts and the hierarchy of legal systems set in place to ensure law and order. No, this is a small, everyday kind of justice, a lowercase justice, we might say. Or, as we push our thinking even further, we might say it's an unconventional dispensing of justice that's described in an unconventional way. Subversive acts are taking place in the action *and* in the telling.

In this way we can say that the textual choices were far from arbitrary. They were, in fact, highly purposeful, adding dimensions of complexity and meaning that wouldn't have been there if the piece had been written in any other way. And we find ourselves full of admiration and astonishment for what the author has managed to achieve and for what we were able to see, though we must acknowledge that we wouldn't have seen this much if we hadn't taken the time, if we hadn't lingered, and while lingering, tried to name what we noticed in language.

We also must acknowledge that our reading of "justice" is informed by the many students and teachers we've shared the piece with through the years. One of the joys of this kind of inquiry is that someone always sees something in a piece of writing that we haven't noticed before in a way that expands and enriches our own thinking and deepens our understanding. And as we try to articulate our thoughts, questioning if a piece made us feel this way or that, entertaining more than one possibility, we open doors that push our thinking further and lead us to more than we previously knew. There is true pleasure in reading this way, true pleasure and satisfaction. We urge you to try it with a colleague, your students, or right here beside us.

From Inquiry to Apprenticeship

We have seen how conducting an inquiry into a rule-breaking text can lead to a deeper understanding both of the need for traditional punctuation and grammar and of the effects that can be achieved by purposefully abandoning conventions. In the previous inquiry we chart all the lessons we learned from the piece, both through direct instruction (e.g., punctuation is a navigational tool) and through the class's collaborative thinking. This way all students have public access to the discoveries of the inquiry and can refer to them as desired or needed. Such a chart might look like this:

What We've Learned from Studying "justice"

- Writers use punctuation to help their readers make their way through texts that would otherwise be confusing.
- Writers use punctuation to help their readers interpret what they're reading in a more artistic or insightful way.
- Writers sometimes choose to break the rules for specific purposes.
- Writers often think about *how* they're going to say what they want to say so that the form or structure of their piece reinforces or mirrors the content.

Two small but significant details to note: When we talk to students or synthesize information for them in written form, such as on charts, we try to use the term *writer* or *writers* instead of an author's given name in order to underscore the notion that these are matters all writers consider, not just this particular one. And this makes the ideas more transferable from one piece to another. We also write our charts in class, even though we know they'd be neater and more organized if we did them by ourselves. But we want to solicit our students' ideas as we write so that the chart, too, becomes a group effort, the result of our collaborative thinking. This means, though, that the chart in one room may look slightly different from the chart in another embarked on the same study—or even from a chart in the same room that was written with a different group of students—because we want to use the particular language that emerges in each class's discussions in order to make the information more accessible and meaningful.

One question that remains, though, is How do students then take what they've learned and incorporate it into their own writing? The answer, we believe, is through experimental apprenticeship. With a text such as "justice," we do not ask students to mentor themselves word for word and phrase for phrase, as we do in the following chapter. Instead we ask them to consider the lessons they'd learned from the piece and play around with them, in particular to see if they could break the rules in a way that both supported the meaning of the piece and reminded us of punctuation's purpose. Depending on how much scaffolding the class seems to need (e.g., do they seem eager and ready to try it? Are their pencils and notebooks in hand? Or are they looking at us like we're crazy?), we might show them precisely what this looks like by trying to model it ourselves. If they seem to need less than a full demonstration but could use a bit of a jump start, we might also ask them to brainstorm with us the kinds of actions, events, or incidents that might be suited to an unconventional telling. Asked to do this, students that we've worked with have come up with things like nightmares, daydreams, tricks and cons, insomnia, roller coasters—all things that involve the kind of disorientation we felt in the mentor piece.

If we have been carefully observing our students, assessing their understanding as we went and not leaving any pertinent teaching point until we were sure that at least most of them got it, we would have a good idea at that point of what they were capable of, though always it is best to be prepared for any contingency. Let's say, for instance, that we have a class that, indeed, has been seduced by rodriguez's piece. There's been a definite buzz in the room, from the moment we first introduced the piece right through the whole business of charting. They've followed us through a complicated text and surprised us with the depth of their insights. In fact, they've seemed so eager and excited that we've had to rein them in a bit just so they wouldn't start to write prematurely. But now it is our best opinion that they're ready to do it alone, and so we give them the maximum amount of time and encouragement to try. We review the discoveries we previously charted and reiterate what we're asking them to do: to try writing something that breaks the rules in a purposeful way. Then we send them off without further ado. "Go ahead," we say, "have a go at it and then we'll share what happened."

Imagine, too, that they rush to their seats with that same kind of verve and energy, having already sharpened their pencils and turned to a new notebook page. But as we wander around the room, looking over students' shoulders and conferring, we see that many students seem stymied. They are sitting there with heads cradled in hands, staring off into space, doing nothing more with their freshly sharpened pencils than absently chewing on them. We sense, with a growing feeling of dismay, that we've overestimated what they could do and have set our expectations too high. We feel defeat and failure nudging at us and may even be tempted to blame our students, to say it's their fault and not ours. But instead of abandoning our entire plan or plowing on gamely till the end—knowing that things will only get worse if we don't intervene soon—we make a quick decision to change course, gathering up all but the few students who seem to be on a roll to offer additional support. We begin by acknowledging the difficulty of the task and how frustrated they must feel. We even share the frustration we've felt when faced with the sobering realization that our ability to appreciate the effects of other writers is far ahead of our ability to replicate them ourselves. Then we return to our other options, the ones we decided they didn't need. We brainstorm events and situations that might lend themselves to this kind of writing, asking those students who are already off and running what they are working on. And we're pleased to see that more than half the group now feel that they have a place to start. As for the rest, we say, "Don't worry. Maybe you'll be inspired by what some of the others have written. Or maybe you'll want to try it down the line. For now, though, you're free to go back to what you were working on before; though as you write, we want you try to think about how punctuation might help your readers understand your piece more clearly, and maybe even try to use it as a way to support your mood or tone."

We do it this way because, while we do want students to stretch themselves and expand their repertoire as writers, we believe that choice and ownership are critical to a writing workshop's success and that the tone created through support and respect is ultimately more likely to encourage risk taking than forcing students to undertake tasks they might not be ready to tackle yet. For now, though, let's leave this imagined class behind and move on to closely look at how one student actually used the mentor text to create a powerful piece of writing.

A Case Study in Apprenticeship

Dan was a seventh grader at a Manhattan middle school that, like virtually all New York City schools, comprised a diverse population. Many of the students were fluent readers and writers, though many others were not, and Dan was one of the latter. He was born in Korea and had learned English as a second language in grade school, though it seemed unclear just how much he knew since, in class, he remained mostly silent. He rarely participated in classroom discussions and seemed to struggle with his writing, hardly ever bringing anything he did to the point of publication. In fact, his notebook seemed downright bereft, filled with only some cursory freewriting and some doodles in the margins. He was also overweight and nonathletic, which, combined with his questionable grasp of English and the awkwardness of being thirteen, made him seem like a boy who, if given the choice, might opt for invisibility. And we knew the risk that boys like Dan run of being discounted or forgotten about, left alone to fend for themselves, the victims of expectations that have been lowered.

As a whole, the class responded to "justice" with much enthusiasm. The students clearly saw how adding punctuation made the piece accessible and readable in a way that it hadn't first seemed, though they also could verbalize how much they thought was gained by the author's decision to leave it out. Having been schooled to identify themes, they decided that the theme of the piece was anarchy, and it truly gave them satisfaction and pleasure to realize how the theme manifested itself not just in the content but in the form. The piece, they saw, was anarchistic in every sort of way, and this definitely made them appreciate it more—though it was hard to say with Dan, who sat through the class in his typical fashion: silent and seemingly inattentive.

Yet this is the piece that Dan wrote that day, using "justice" as a mentor text:

> In class I sit on the side with my friend Warren. I am very quiet in class. So many kids are talking. They don't need me to talk. They just keep talking. They like to hear their own voices. It doesn't matter what we are talking about. It is always the same people. How could the same people always have something important to say about every thing? I put my chin in my hand and I have a look on my face so it looks like I am listening. It's important in class to look like you are listening. Inside my head though, it is different.

inside my head there is a band playing with saxophones and trombones and maybe an oboe and a clarinet it is a jazz band where everybody improvises but only when they have something to say then that player lets loose a melody and others listen and then they just pick it up too but always remembering that first melody and how it started them all on this musical ride it is a wild rollercoaster of sound and hear comes the drummer now look out

The teacher yells at me to stop tapping my pencil. Oh, and she is upset because I don't seem to be listening.

Dan's writing disrupts the notion that his silence and his difficulties with writing were rooted in his shaky hold on English. Here he is telling us that he has understood many things, and not just about English and grammar. He knows how certain classrooms operate, and he knows how to conform, though he knows, as well, that the conformity's a sham, a superficial posing. He knows about power and the forms that support it. And he knows something about anarchy and music.

In terms of grammar, we see how Dan has absorbed both the grammatical lessons from "justice" as well as its anarchist spirit, while thoroughly making the piece *his*. It is not an imitation as much as an offshoot, a variation on a theme, in which he has borrowed what he learned from rodriguez to create something original and new. He has found a perfect subject for purposeful rule breaking. Jazz, with its experimentations and its rangy, unruly sound, is a kind of aural equivalent to unpunctuated prose; it is wild and free, not subject to the rules of more conventional music. It is subversive just as Dan's piece is, pushing the limits of melody and rhythm just as Dan pushes the boundaries of grammar. And just as we can lose ourselves in jazz, in the ever-changing tempos and rhythms, we lose ourselves in Dan's middle section, which is like a riff that we're carried through on a swift, pulsing current of words.

But Dan has done something else in this piece that rodriguez didn't attempt. He has posited the world of improvisation against the world of the classroom, where rules and "correct" behavior matter and where students are expected to conform to certain, preset expectations about what it means to listen and learn, just as sentences are expected to conform to a prescribed standard of correctness. And the restrictive nature of that classroom world is reinforced and reflected by the grammatical choices Dan has made. Sentences in those sections are short and declarative. The punctuation is utilitarian, limited mostly to periods and a lone question mark, though commas, which suggest more subtle relationships, make a cameo appearance in two strategic places. The first occurs as we segue from the classroom to the world inside Dan's head, where it seems to alert us that we're moving away from that straightforward, cut-and-dried world, and heading to a place more complicated and nuanced, more equivocal and paradoxical. The other appears in the very last sentence, where it seems to signal an aside, a casual, oh-by-the-way remark that's tossed in at the last minute. But this, too, seems purposeful and, in fact, quite sly, for the piece itself is clearly proof that Dan has been listening and learning. He has absorbed the lessons that were taught so thoroughly that he's able to apply them in ways we hadn't envisioned to the degree that this piece can now stand and act as a mentor text itself—where, in addition to the many things about grammar it can teach us, we might also look at how Dan skillfully uses white space, particularly near the end, where without actually saying so, we know that he's been tapping his pencil on his desk, drumming to the beat inside his head, so absorbed and oblivious that he's heard nothing else until the teacher starts screaming.

But was Dan really conscious of all the effects we've noted and given him credit for? Probably not, or at least not in the sophisticated way that we've described them here. Similarly, we can't claim to know rodriguez's true intentions, but it is fruitful to speculate, to imagine the choices that writers make so that students better understand the deliberation process. In terms of Dan, though, it is clear that he's capable of far more than first may have been thought. He clearly meant to juxtapose one world against the other, and he clearly understood that manipulating the grammar, so that it was limited and rigid in the first part and free-form in the second, would make the juxtaposition more powerful. He also realized that for the piece to work, his grammar in the first and last paragraphs had to conform to traditional rules, and this provided him with a real reason for taking on work he'd never taken on before. He was invested in making sure that his sentences were sentences, that his periods were in the right place. No fragments or run-ons should appear here, no misplaced question marks, not simply because fragments or run-ons were "wrong," but because he sensed they would undermine what he was trying to achieve. And as for the commas, while we doubt that he considered the full impact of the commas as we did when we lingered as readers, we do believe that when students are really engaged with language to this degree—when they are really digging in and thinking about word choice, punctuation, sentences—unexpected things can happen. Connections and surprises begin to appear beyond what the author intended or even is aware of, though they are there for readers to discover and delight in, like small, hidden gems. And they are there for writers to appreciate, as well, when they're pointed out.

Fitting Experimentation In: Some Ideas on Unit Planning

Dan's piece stands as a testament to what can actually happen when you present children with provocative ideas that are carefully scaffolded to make them accessible and then give them the time and the space and the encouragement to practice and experiment. The piece is also a persuasive indictment against traditional pedagogy; one can only imagine that when Dan turns to his next piece of writing, he will carry with him a greater and more subtle understanding of punctuation and grammar than any worksheet or drill could have given him. And it acts as a cautionary tale, as well, reminding us of the constant need to not underestimate our students. Additionally, the act of apprenticeship liberated Dan's voice, connecting him with writing in a way that none of our prompts had done before. We can chart for ourselves all the lessons, we as teachers, have learned from Dan:

- Sometimes conventional grammar does little to augment student voice.
- Some students find voice in subversive forms.
- Contrasting conventional and subversive subjects and language is an art.
- Sometimes teachers have only little knowledge of their students' capacities.
- Some students experience school, and English, as oppressive forces.
- Students are capable of lively resistance.

But where do we fit this kind of work in during our busy day, with books to read and tests to prepare for and genres to explore in writing? One way we've done it is to create a unit that specifically looks at how and when writers purposefully break rules in a way that encourages experimentation but also provides students with a better understanding of what purpose the rules actually serve. We turn now to describe one such unit as a case study.

At one Manhattan high school, for instance, we designed a six-week unit for ninth graders that we called Grammar and Voice. The unit was developed out of a frustration expressed at an English department meeting that students needed more instruction in grammar and there seemed no room in the busy curriculum to possibly fit it in. Fortunately, though, the school had in place a writing arts class for ninth and tenth graders to help them make the transition to high school and its more rigorous expectations. So in addition to their literature-based English class, which met five times a week, each ninth and tenth grader took a writing arts class three periods a week. The class was run as a workshop, with the year divided into genre-based units. Already that year the ninth graders had studied and written personal essays, had completed a collaborative multi-genre project that supported the school's commitment to group work, and had just begun to study feature articles. For every unit, we had identified an instructional focus for grammar—for example, we looked at paragraphs with the essay, dialogue punctuation with feature articles—though with all that needed to be taught with each genre, the grammar minilessons were almost inevitably squeezed in during revision.

We had also noted that, while students for the most part incorporated those lessons in the pieces they were working on, the lessons didn't always transfer from one unit to the next, raising yet again the problematic question of retention. And so, working closely with the writing arts teacher, we planned an in-depth grammar unit that incorporated rule-breaking work in order to raise the students' awareness and sensitivity to grammar in a way that would encourage habits of mind. And we decided to link grammar with a study of voice—how writers use syntax and punctuation to create powerful voices—as a way to make it seem both less dry and, we hoped, more engaging.

We began planning first by identifying which elements of grammar we wanted to explore, knowing that it would be foolhardy to try to be encyclopedic. And we decided, for our pilot year, to focus on three things: punctuation, sentence fragments, and run-ons. We would save a look at verbs and more syntax options for the following year, when we hoped to implement part 2 in the students' sophomore year. We also consulted two books in the field, Harry Noden's *Image Grammar* (1999), which gave us some marvelous lesson ideas that we put into practice, and *Breaking the Rules*, by Edgar Schuster (2003), whose extensively researched investigation into current usage trends and the efficacy—or lack thereof—of traditional grammar instruction confirmed we were on the right track. And we brainstormed possible final assessments, deciding that we would ask each student to create a small anthology consisting of two or three short pieces that had been written in response to the unit's explorations. In these pieces, students would be encouraged to break as many rules as they liked on the condition that they could defend their choices as part of a meaningful plan. Thus each piece in the anthology would be accompanied by a short reflective piece in which the students would articulate what effects they were trying to achieve and how they thought using fragments and run-ons and different kinds of punctuation helped them. This would also allow students whose understanding of effects in reading surpassed their ability to duplicate them in writing to demonstrate their knowledge. Credit would be given for intention and effort, not just for proficiency, since we knew that mastery was something not everyone could achieve at the same time.

Additionally, as a concession to the other English teachers, who feared that opening the door to rule breaking would only reinforce misconceptions and bad habits, we agreed to also ask the students to write a more a traditional version of each piece where fragments would be reconfigured as whole sentences and more standard punctuation would apply. This way we would ensure that any rule breaking was indeed purposeful and that the students, say, were not simply writing run-ons because they didn't recognize them as such.

Thus with all our goals defined and set, we mapped out the following initial calendar:

Week 1—A First Look at Punctuation as Readers: Teaching student writers ways to appreciate punctuation by seeing how it can alter meaning and serve artistic ends

Week 2—Mentoring to Punctuation Texts as Writers: Experimenting in Notebooks: Exploring how writers break the rules of punctuation to create powerful effects and trying to do it too

Week 3—A Look at Fragments as Readers and Writers: More Notebook Experimentation: Looking at fragments to understand why they are, indeed, fragments and then exploring how writers use them to achieve particular effects

Week 4—A Look at Run-ons as Readers and Writers: More Notebook Experimentation: Looking at run-ons to understand why they are run-ons and not full sentences and then exploring how writers use them to achieve particular effects

Week 5—Introduction of Final Project: Drafting: Giving students their final project assignments and spending much class time working on them and conferring with peers and teachers

Week 6—Final Projects: Revision and Editing: Continuing to work on the anthologies, revising and editing

We then turned to the task of hunting for texts. We knew we wanted to use "justice" as a mentor, and we had a few more up our sleeves (several of which we'll share later), but we realized we didn't have many samples of writers using run-ons purposely. But what we did find were wordy sentences—sentences with a slew of *and*s or with endless strings of clauses—the kind of sentences that were technically correct, in the sense of having a subject and a predicate, but which were often subjected, when found in student writing, to the teacher's red pen. These seemed definitely worth looking at, as writers seemed to write them all the time, and we thought how we could use them to support student thinking about what constitutes a sentence by taking a sentence that was meandering and rambling and seeing if, in fact, it had those two components, a subject and a predicate.

This did, though, necessitate our first revision: week 4 would be devoted to wordy sentences, not run-ons, with the term *run-on* introduced when the students looked at "justice." Then with this adjustment in place, we began to think of the actual lessons we would teach, day by day and week to week, knowing as we plotted this out that we might have to tinker once again with our original calendar.

Thus the process we went through to plan the unit consisted of the following steps:

1. Identify the unit's goals and objectives in terms of what enduring understandings we want students to come away with (i.e., to raise students' aware-

ness and sensitivity to the effects of, and the purposes behind, the grammatical choices that writers make when they write).

2. Identify the specific elements within the world of grammar that we want to address (punctuation, sentence fragments, and wordy sentences).

3. Consult professional texts to aid our thinking so that we don't have to reinvent the wheel (*Image Grammar* and *Breaking the Rules*).

4. Envision and define a final project that will act as an assessment tool to measure the students' new skills and understanding (an anthology comprising three parts: a handful of pieces in which students try to manipulate grammar to achieve particular effects, a reflective piece to accompany each of the above, stating the author's purpose and how the choices he or she made supported those purposes, and a piece that translates each rule-breaking text into one with more conventional usage).

5. Map out a week-by-week calendar (as shown earlier).

6. Look for, and decide on, mentor texts and consider how they support or alter our initial planning.

7. Craft the actual minilessons we will teach each week using the mentor texts and other lesson ideas derived from professional texts.

8. Make whatever adjustments might be needed to our original calendar now that we've mapped out the lessons.

9. Be prepared to rethink and reflect on our planning if the students don't seem to be with us.

These steps can be followed to plan all kinds of units, such as genre units and author studies, though perhaps the most critical are the first and last. It is imperative to take the time to articulate what it is we want students to learn, not just in terms of facts and skills, but in terms of the broader understandings they will carry with them throughout life, in order to provide a clear focus for our instruction. And it is important that we recognize that even the most thoughtfully and thoroughly planned lesson must be judged not by how it looks or sounds on paper, or even how well it is executed, but by how well it manages to promote student learning, which is the ultimate goal.

And so with plans in hand and minds still thinking, we finally started the unit.

Launching the Unit: Week 1

Given that these were ninth graders who, for better or worse, had been the recipients of grammar instruction for at least a half dozen years, we decided not to bog down our initial session with too much talk about the functions of individual punctuation marks. They knew, after all, what a period was and could recognize semicolons, though they didn't always know how to use them effectively even though they'd been "taught." Instead, we wanted them to come away from that first week with a deeper understanding of how all punctuation affects meaning in both obvious and more subtle ways, how it acts as both a navigational tool and an artistic one. So we borrowed an idea from Harry Noden (1999, 187) and bought ourselves a copy of *Anguished English*, by Richard Lederer (1987), an anthology, so the cover claims, "of accidental assaults upon our language." The book is filled with malapropisms and all sorts of grammatical gaffes that Lederer has collected over the years from both student and professional writers, including sentences like "Medieval cathedrals were supported by flying buttocks," and actually published headlines such as "Grandmother of Eight Makes Hole in One."

For our inquiry purposes, we combed through the book looking for sentences whose intended meaning was altered or subverted—often to hilarious effects—by the misuse or absence of punctuation marks. While we would never teach using student writing as negative examples, here we do look at what happens when punctuation goes awry in published pieces in order to demonstrate how closely punctuation is linked to meaning. A few we put on a overhead for the whole class to look at during the minilesson, while the rest we wrote out on strips of paper to be handed out to groups of students for more independent work. Thus, on the first day of our new unit we put this sentence up on the overhead and asked students to think about what it actually said as opposed to what it presumably meant to say:

> As a baboon who grew up wild in the jungle, I realized that Wiki had special nutritional needs.

Interestingly, the students saw nothing wrong with the sentence when they first read it. They knew that Wiki was a baboon and that she had special nutritional needs, but they didn't at first see that what it actually said was that the author was a baboon who grew up in the jungle, and because he had that background, he realized that Wiki—who could be anything or anyone—had special nutritional needs. We could say that they misread it because they read too quickly or didn't pay enough attention. Or we could wonder if, perhaps, our minds are hardwired for making meaning, and through some compensating neurological process, they instinctively knew what the author meant and simply read it that way, ignoring what didn't make sense. Either way, though, we pointed out to students the gap between what the author meant to say and what was really on the page, and we showed how the sentence could be refigured so that it said what it meant, by writing either *As a baboon who grew up wild in the jungle, Wiki had special nutritional needs* or, if we wanted to preserve the realization embedded in the original sentence, *I realized that Wiki, the baboon, had special nutritional needs because she'd grown up wild in the jungle.*

Then we threw up another example and tried it again, asking the same question: What does the sentence actually say as opposed to its intended meaning?

> She watched as her father returned home with the horses all dressed in cowboy attire.

This time the students were catching on, and we had an amusing moment or two imagining horses dressed in Stetsons and chaps. But they still had trouble recasting the sentence so it said what it meant to say. After one more try with support, though, they seemed to be getting the hang of it, and we decided that they were ready for more independent work. So we broke them into small groups, giving each group another sentence that they had to read carefully for meaning as we'd done as a whole class. We also passed out a piece of chart paper on which we asked them to write down the original sentence and the sentence or sentences they composed to convey the true meaning of what the original sentence had mangled. Then they would present their findings to the class as a whole, sharing both what they thought the original sentence actually said, as opposed to what it meant to say, and how they would recast it to make sure that the meaning was clear.

We knew the lesson was successful, at least in terms of engagement, when we heard first laughter and giggles erupt as the groups keyed in to the ridiculousness of what their mangled sentences actually said and then silence, as they attempted to rewrite for clearer meaning. Some groups even decided to illustrate their work with a comic-book-style drawing of the often hilarious or outrageous thing their original sentence said. And their presentations were marked as well by laughter that gave way to seriousness as they explained the choices they made to clarify each sentence's confusions.

All in all, we felt the students left the room that day with a deeper understanding of how punctuation creates and clarifies meaning—all without a single mention of rules. Next we wanted them to begin to explore the way that punctuation creates other effects that more subtly and artistically support meaning. And for this we adapted another idea from Noden (1999, 106). In order to help students understand how punctuation is often discretionary, based less on the strict adherence to rules than on how a writer wants his reader to feel, we presented the students with an unpunctuated page of text and asked them to punctuate it. Again we thought they should work in groups, since we imagined the assignment would be difficult and might benefit from minds working together. And for texts, we decided to use the first page from the contemporary novels they had recently finished reading in book groups, hoping thereby to make a connection between the English and writing rooms and also to draw on some of the enthusiasm they felt for their book-group books.

Before we let them loose on the task, though, we set the stage slightly differently than Noden does. Instead of arming them with a punctuation hierarchy that looks at the different levels of separation that punctuation creates and how those separations relate to the pauses that create a piece of prose's rhythm (e.g., periods for maximum separation, semicolons for a medium one), we wanted to kick off the lesson by aligning punctuation to more emotional or psychological effects. So we shared with them the final paragraph of Pico Iyer's essay "In Praise of the Humble Comma":

> Punctuation, then, is a matter of care. Care for words, yes, but also, and more important, for what the words imply. Only a lover notices the small things: the way the afternoon light catches the nape of a neck, or how a strand of hair slips out from behind an ear, or the way a finger curls around a cup. And no one scans a letter so closely as a lover, searching for its small print, straining to hear its nuances, its gasps, its sighs and hesitations, poring over the secret messages that lie in every cadence. The difference between "Jane (whom I adore)" and "Jane, whom I adore," and the difference between them both and "Jane—whom I adore—" marks all the distance between ecstasy and heartache

. . . Punctuation, in fact, is a labor of love. Which brings us back, in a way, to gods. (1996, 82)

We asked the students to read the piece silently so that they weren't affected by the meaning that we, ourselves, might naturally convey through the intonation of our voice, and then we asked them to consider those three phrases about Jane. Which one did they think conveyed heartache and which one suggested ecstasy? And what did they think the one left conveyed in the grand spectrum of feelings? We asked them to discuss this with a partner then offer their thoughts to the class. And while there was some lively disagreement, the consensus was that *Jane (whom I adore)* seemed to speak to heartbreak because the isolation of the phrase in parentheses suggested that it might be too painful to utter if it weren't somehow contained, while *Jane—whom I adore—* seemed ecstatic because the dashes seemed extravagant, more reflective of someone madly in love. Or as one student said, "The dashes were dashing," and that seemed more related to ecstasy than heartache. On the other hand, *Jane, whom I adore,* (which uses the most common punctuation) seemed emotionally more neutral. It was stated as a fact, something that was a given, though without being able to name it precisely, the students circled around the idea that there was something a bit patronizing about it, something a little dismissive, that, we suggested, they might not feel if the author just said, "I adore Jane."

We were impressed with what they came up with but still thought they might need more support before we set them loose, and so we put an unpunctuated version of the first page of *Catcher in the Rye* on the overhead and modeled for them the exact kind of thinking we wanted them to do. We tried to determine where one sentence ended and another one began and debated over what punctuation to use based on our understanding of Holden Caulfield as a character and how we now were beginning to see punctuation affect meaning and voice and tone. And we shared our thinking aloud with the students, articulating what we thought were the pros and cons of using a semicolon instead of a period or the effects we thought might be achieved by setting a phrase off in dashes. Then after a while we invited the students to join us in this decision making, and while this was clearly difficult for them—responding to effects already on the page being easier than actually creating them—we decided, when we reached the end of the page, to see what they could do on their own, even if they would have to struggle.

So we put them in groups and passed out the pages of unpunctuated text, and we circled the room offering encouragement by acknowledging that what we'd asked was hard but that we knew they would get better at it the more they practiced and tried. We had also told them that when they were finished, we would give them a copy of the punctuated text as it appeared in print, so they could compare their decisions with the author's, and we noted how that triggered some anxiety, as if we were giving them a test. So we had to additionally reassure them that there was no right or wrong way to do this, provided they could explain their thinking by articulating the meaning they thought their choices conveyed and the effects they created.

And with this encouragement and clarification, we overheard some wonderful conversations, like the one from the group that was intently working on this passage from Robert Corimer's *I Am the Cheese* ([1977] 1997):

> I am riding the bicycle and I am on Route 31 in Monument Massachusetts on my way to Rutterburg Vermont and I am pedaling furiously because this is an old-fashioned bike no speeds no fenders only the warped tires and the brakes that don't always work and the handlebars with cracked rubber grips to steer with a plain bike the kind my father rode as a kid years ago it's cold as I pedal along the wind like a snake slithering up my sleeves and into my jacket and my pant legs too but I keep pedaling I keep pedaling

After spending some time wracking their brains to see what they remembered about commas and places (i.e., they knew that there had to be a comma between the towns and states, but was there one after the states as well?), they moved on to more meaningful matters. They decided they wanted to come up with punctuation that would somehow convey how furiously the narrator was pedaling and that might somehow mimic the act of pedaling itself, the unending round-and-round of it. They knew, for instance, that there "should" be a period between the first *I keep pedaling* and the last, but they thought that wouldn't completely convey the cyclical nature of pedaling, and so they decided to use a comma instead. And hearing them seriously debate the merits of dashes and commas and periods almost brought tears to our eyes.

Ultimately this is how they decided to punctuate the piece:

I am riding the bicycle, and I am on Route 31 in Monument, Massachusetts, on my way to Rutterburg, Vermont, and I am pedaling furiously because this is an old-fashioned bike—no speeds, no fenders, only the warped tires and the brakes that don't always work and the handlebars with cracked rubber grips to steer with. A plain bike, the kind my father rode as a kid years ago. It's cold as I pedal along, the wind like a snake slithering up my sleeves and into my jacket and my pant legs too, but I keep pedaling, I keep pedaling:

This is not too far from how Corimer did it himself, probably for the same reasons:

I am riding the bicycle and I am on Route 31 in Monument, Massachusetts, on my way to Rutterburg, Vermont, and I am pedaling furiously because this is an old-fashioned bike, no speeds, no fenders, only the warped tires and the brakes that don't always work and the handlebars with cracked rubber grips to steer with. A plain bike—the kind my father rode as a kid years ago. It's cold as I pedal along, the wind like a snake slithering up my sleeves and into my jacket and my pant legs, too. But I keep pedaling, I keep pedaling.

After they had reached some kind of decision, we gave each group two overheads, one of the text as it appeared in the book and one that was unpunctuated, and once again we asked the students to present their work to the class as a whole, in order to give them additional practice at articulating their choices. Watching them explain their choices, and seeing how well they were beginning to grasp the connection between a sentence's content and form made us feel quite successful, though we knew that the true challenge lay ahead, when we would ask students to keep this in mind as they wrote themselves, applying the idea not after the fact on somebody else's work, but actually as they composed. But at least, for now, at the end of week 1, we thought we were on the right track. And so we embarked on week 2 with much hope.

First Attempts at Apprenticeship: Week 2

We have spelled out in detail how we've used "justice" in a classroom, and we followed that method closely here as well. Before we turned to it, however, we showed the students another piece that broke certain rules to powerful effects without doing so quite so radically. The piece, by Debra Marquart, is titled "Getting Ready," and we present it here as it appears in *Welcome to Your Life*:

i'm the thousand-change girl, getting ready for school,
standing in my bedroom ripping pants and shirts from my
body, trying dresses and skirts. father, at the bottom
of the steps is yelling, the bus is coming, here comes
the bus. i'm wriggling into jeans—zippers grinding their teeth,
buttons refusing their holes. my brother, dressed-
in-five-minutes, stands in the hall, t-shirt and bookbag,
saying what's the big problem. i'm kneeling in front of
the closet, foraging for that great-lost-other-shoe.
father, downstairs, offers advice. slacks, he's yelling,
just put on some slacks. i'm in the mirror, matching
earrings, nervous fingers putting the back to the front.
downstairs, the bus is fuming in the yard, farm kids
with cowlicks sitting in rows. everything's in a pile
on the floor. after school, mother will scream, get upstairs
and hang up that mess, but i don't care, i'm the thousand-
change girl, trotting downstairs now looking good, looking
ready for school. father, pulling back from the steps with
disgust, giving me the once over, saying, is *that*
what you're wearing? (1998, 63)

We love this piece for its immediacy and its sassy, spunky voice, and the students loved it too, though we needed to prod them and push them a bit to get them to articulate why. Just why, we asked—aside from the content, which many of the students related to—is the piece so appealing? The students spoke of its freshness and quirkiness—what we called spunk and sass—and saw that it was there, not just in what Marquart said, but again, in how she said it. They pointed to the way she dispensed with all capitals and quotation marks as if she couldn't be bothered with them, just as the narrator can't be bothered by the clothes that are piling up on the floor. And the narrator made things her own by the way she named them, like her brother, for instance, Mr. Dressed-in-Five-Minutes, and the great-lost-other-shoe. And when asked to look specifically at the verbs, they could see there was something inventive there too, with zippers grinding, buttons refusing holes, and school buses fuming in the yard. One student said that was personification, and we acknowledged he was right, though we said we were less interested in naming it than in seeing what it achieved—what we described as a kind of crackling energy, as though everything the narrator touched was alive and there to be engaged in; we could imagine her finding that great-lost-other-shoe and embracing it like a long lost friend—or, conversely, we could picture her wagging her finger, scolding it like a naughty child.

Because the piece had sparked so much discussion and seemed so accessible, we decided to forego the modeling we had planned and even decided to postpone the charting until we gave the class a chance to try writing like Marquart first. The only thing we requested was this: that they keep the piece in front of them while they wrote, not in order to follow it word by word or line by line, but to keep the voice she created by playing around with punctuation and language right there in their heads. Then, while the students wrote, we wandered through the room, taking notes and occasionally conferring, though only a few students seemed to hesitate or be puzzled; most just sank right in. And since we had billed this as a time to experiment, we didn't want to interrupt the flow to talk about matters of craft yet, so we spent our time peering over shoulders and offering words of encouragement.

One thing we did note, though, which surprised us and seemed to speak to the power of apprenticeship, was that, while we had spoken at great length before about how writers often write small, zooming in and freezing moments they then explode by writing with evocative, sensory detail, those lessons seemed hit-or-miss. Some students got it and some students didn't, though we spoke of it again and again. Yet here, with the mentor text right in front them, they all were lingering, catching small but telling details that brought the moment they were writing of alive, without us having mentioned it once. They seemed to just do it independently, as part of their apprenticeship work, absorbing other lessons from the text that they applied to their work.

The following day we looked at "justice," and while the conversation around it was as provocative as it had been at Dan's school, the same thing happened when we asked the students to write. Some clearly felt inspired and took off right away, while others seemed perplexed. And after helping some of the latter get started, we gave the others permission to go back to "Getting Ready" and either keep working on what they had started the day before or try on that voice again with a different subject matter.

And then it was on to week 3.

Continued Apprenticeship: Weeks 3 and 4

For many years, educators and writers like Tom Romano (1995, 1999, 2004) have been calling our attention to the power of sentence fragments, pointing out how frequently they make an appearance in the world of literature, despite the fact that in most classrooms their use is absolutely verboten. Some teachers see them only as proof that a student doesn't know what a sentence is, not as a sign that the student might be trying to use them purposely to create an effect. And students often feel this way, too. When we polled the students about sentence fragments on the first day of week 3, they defined them as something that wasn't a full sentence, and they labeled them as wrong. They were constructions that needed correction, since something in them was missing, though the students couldn't remember what that missing thing was called until we offered the words *subject* and *predicate* and some of them nodded their heads. Then we passed out an excerpt from another text and asked them to silently read it, underlining any sentence fragments they happened to come across. The passage was from Jean Fritz's memoir, *Homesick* (1982), a book that many had read or heard in lower school and now remembered fondly. And it was a book, we pointed out, that was so universally respected and admired that it won the American Book Award and was named a Newbery Honor Book.

In my father's study there was a large globe with all the countries of the world running around it. I could put my finger on the exact spot where I was and had been ever since I'd been born. And I was on the wrong side of the globe. I was in China in a city named Hankow, a dot on a crooked line that seemed to break the country right in two. The line was really the Yangtse River, but who would know by looking at a map what the Yangtse River really was?

Orange-brown, muddy mustard-colored. And wide, wide, wide. With a river smell that was old and came all the way up from the bottom. Sometimes old women knelt on the riverbank, begging the River God to return a son or grandson who may have drowned. They would wail and beat the earth to make the River God pay attention, but I knew how busy the River God must be. All those people on the Yangtse River! Coolies hauling water. Women washing clothes. Houseboats swarming with old people and young, chickens and pigs. Big crooked-sailed junks with eyes painted on their prows so they could see where they were going. I loved the Yangtse River, but, of course, I belonged on the other side of the world. In America, with my grandmother. (9)

For most of the students, the task was easy. Finding fragments when you're looking for them, particularly in some else's work, proved to be not all that hard, and they readily saw that the second paragraph was chock-full of them. But why, we asked, did the author write them if they were considered wrong? Was it just a slip of her pen that went unnoticed, not only by her but by her editor, her publisher, the book award juries? That, of course, did not seem likely; we assumed that she put them there on purpose. And so the question we now posed was, What effects did she achieve by using fragments when she did?

To help the students grapple with this question, we thought it might be helpful to hear how the piece might sound if those fragments were recast as whole sentences. Thus, interactively, we rewrote the second paragraph so that it looked like this:

> The Yangtse River was orange-brown and muddy mustard-colored. It was wide, wide, wide, with a river smell that was old and came all the way up from the bottom. Sometimes old women knelt on the riverbank, begging the River God to return a son or grandson who may have drowned. They would wail and beat the earth to make the River God pay attention, but I knew how busy the River God must be. There were so many people on the Yangtse River! There were coolies hauling water. There were women washing clothes. There were houseboats swarming with old people and young, chickens and pigs. There were big crooked-sailed junks with eyes painted on their prows so they could see where they were going. I loved the Yangtse River, but, of course, I belonged on the other side of the world, in America, with my grandmother.

Then we compared the two different versions, thinking about what was lost and gained by making the piece conform to standard usage. The students didn't feel that anything was lost by rewriting the first two sentences, though they conceded that all those *there were*s made the piece sound clunky. And drawing on the experience they had in punctuating their book-group texts, a few were able to point to the last sentence and make a case for leaving the *In America . . .* separate, because it reinforced the idea that America was so far away, it wasn't even in the same sentence. Then the fragment was like a continent separated from the sentence before it by a period and a space that suggested the ocean, with the sense of distance and dislocation reinforced by the grammatical choices Fritz made.

Then we shared with them our thinking as well, continuing to model how we talk about texts by trying to articulate both what we notice and how what we notice affects us. Thus, we said that in addition to making the middle clunky, turning the fragments into full sentences made the scene seem less immediate. As it was, the fragments made us feel like all these strange sights were swirling and swarming around us—the coolies, the women, the houseboats, the junks. Each fragment was like a snapshot, capturing an image. In fact, we can almost hear the camera clicking as Fritz tries to capture all she sees. And we imagine how she might, indeed, miss something if she stopped to compose the picture more, framing it within a full sentence. As it is, we sense how exotic and busy the Yangtse River is, and the fragments help us see that, driving home the point once more that writers' choices affect their meaning, even at the level of the sentence.

To give them more time to look at fragments and practice this kind of thinking, we provided the students with a handout on which we'd copied four passages from texts that we thought they'd either know or like and that contained many fragments:

> Four small walls, sheathed in pine, painted white. A window. A door onto the kitchen, for warmth. Two chairs. A bed, nearly filling up the room, like a bird held in cupped hands. Standing by the bed, squire beside his knight, a table bearing a Bible and a lamp. I'm certain you've stood in many such rooms.
>
> Look out the window. That's a sugar maple. Grandfather greatly cherished that tree. Now tilt your head back and look up at the beams. You can still make out the track of his plane. He'd put it, and everything else that would fit, and his wife and baby into a wagon and set out from New Hampshire in the year 1820.
>
> — PAUL FLEISCHMAN, *The Borning Room* (1991, 3)

> This is Brooklyn. Summer. Hot like that with a breeze coming across this block every once in a while. Not enough air to cool anybody. Just to let us know we're still alive. A whole city of us—living and kicking. Walk down any Brooklyn street and there we are. Here I am. Alive. If nothing else, Mama says, we have our lives. Who knows what she means by that.
>
> — JACQUELINE WOODSON, *From the Notebooks of Melanin Sun* (1995, 1)

Yours is the one with mean eyes and a ponytail. Striped swimsuit, stilettos, sunglasses, and gold hoop earrings. Mine is the one with bubble hair. Red swimsuit, stilettos, pearl earrings, and a wire stand. But that's all we can afford, besides one extra outfit apiece. Yours, "Red Flair," sophisticated A-line coatdress with a Jackie Kennedy pillbox hat, white gloves, handbag and heels included. Mine, "Solo in the Spotlight," evening elegance in black glitter strapless gown with a puffy skirt at the bottom like a mermaid tail, formal-length gloves, pink chiffon scarf, and mike included. From so much dressing and undressing, the black glitter wears off where her titties stick out. This and a dress invented from an old sock when we cut holes here and here and here, the cuff rolled over for the glamorous, fancy-free, off-the-shoulder look.

— SANDRA CISNEROS, "Barbie-Q" (1991b, 14)

Tell you just how it was with her. Took her to a dance not long after she comes to live with us. Smartest thing I ever done. Seems like some old Eaglespirit woman saw her living down here and came back just to be with Clarissa.

Five years old she was when she come to us. Some foster kids come with lots of stuff, but she came with everything she had in a paper bag. Some dresses that was too short. A pair of pants barely holding a crotch. A pile of ratty underwear and one new nightgown. Mine was her third foster home in as many months. The agency folks said she was *so-cio-path-ic*. I don't know nothing from that. She just seemed like she was all full up with anger and scaredness like lots of the kids who come to me.

— VICKI SEARS, "Dancer" (1997, 21)

We asked them to study each passage carefully then talk in their groups about why they thought the writer might have used fragments by sharing the effects they had on them as readers. Then once they'd discussed each passage individually, we asked them to think about the fragments in general to see if they could come up with any hypotheses about when and why writers used fragments—or, to put it another way, if they could say what purpose or purposes the sentence fragments served.

Once they'd had time to talk this through, we brought the whole class back together and asked that each group choose a spokesperson who would share and report back on the group's thinking. Virtually all of the groups agreed that many of the fragments painted pictures, as Jean Fritz's had, and that isolating those details in fragments helped them as readers to see the picture more. Additionally, referring back to Jean Fritz, some thought that while her fragments created a sense of life spinning and hurtling by, the fragments in Jacqueline Woodson's piece seemed to capture the heat, as if it was simply too darn hot to take the time and trouble to cast the fragments into whole sentences. In the last sample, too, they also thought the fragments helped established the narrator's voice, a woman who they thought from this brief passage was kindhearted but a bit simple or, as one of the students said, "not very well educated." The fragments made her voice sound authentic, as if she was talking directly to her reader just as she'd speak aloud.

From these reactions we created another chart, similar to the one we'd done with "justice," that outlined what we'd learned about fragments. On it we listed such points as these:

- Writers use fragments to create a sense of immediacy—of the here and now.
- Writers use fragments to create pictures that stand out in a reader's mind.
- Writers use fragments to convey the pacing of an action—to speed things up or to slow things down.
- Writers use fragments to help create a character's or narrator's voice—to make it sound like he or she is speaking.
- Writers use fragments to make readers pay more attention to certain details that are significant.

Having summarized the class's current thinking this way, we then led them to experiment with fragments by offering two options: they could either work on something new—perhaps something inspired by some of the passages and readings we'd looked at—or return to something in their notebooks and try rewriting it using fragments. Thus we underscored that fragments should be considered both in the initial acts of composition (whether drafting or writing in a notebook) and in the act of revision.

Like the writing they'd done in response to Debra Marquart's piece, they took to the task readily, so that the room was unusually quiet, filled only with the hum of work and the scratch of pens on paper. And while they worked, we walked around, observing and conferring, hunkering down with a student or two to share with them how we were affected by the fragments they were using, thereby giving essential feedback in the form of a reader's reaction. Then after another day living with fragments, we moved on to wordy sentences, or what Tom Romano calls "labyrinthine sentences," which he describes this way:

> At the opposite end of the sentence-length continuum from the fragment is the labyrinthine sentence—not a lawless, poorly punctuated run-on sentence, but a finely crafted aggregation of words that weaves in and out, accruing information, riding rhythms of parallel sentence structure, tacking on phrases, clauses, and grammatical absolutes to form a sinuous sentence perfectly suited for some things we might describe or discuss. (1995, 81)

To begin our exploration of wordy sentences, and identify what kinds of purposes they might be perfectly suited to, we put a passage from Charlotte Zolotow's picture book *William's Doll* up on the overhead and asked the students what they thought someone—for example, an English teacher—might say was wrong with it:

> William wanted a doll. He wanted to hug it and cradle it in his arms and give it a bottle and take it to the park and push it in the swing and bring it back home and undress it and put it to bed and pull down the shades and kiss it goodnight and watch its eyes close and then William wanted to wake it up in the morning when the sun came in and start all over again just as though he were its father and it were his child. (1972, 5–8)

Immediately a sea of hands shot up. "The second sentence is too long," they said.

"And it has too many *ands*."

"The writer should have broken that sentence up into a few shorter ones."

We then asked them to consider, as we had with Jean Fritz, that Charlotte Zolotow is a well-known writer, the author of more than seventy books, who is so respected and admired in the field that an award is actually named after her, the Charlotte Zolotow Award, which is given each year to the author of the best picture book published in the United States. "So what gives?" we asked the class. "Why did she write it that way?" And seeing a conspicuous absence of hands, we offered the following suggestion: that they turn to a partner and think about whether there might be a possible connection between what the passage is about and how it's been written.

When we then returned to a full-class discussion, many hands went up, all from students who, in one way or another, said that the story was about a boy who really wanted a doll and the sentence that they'd at first deemed wrong helped convey how badly he wanted it, how many ways he wanted it, how multifaceted was his desire. It captured the depth and the breadth of his longing, which was as long as the sentence. As Pico Iyer said earlier, there is heartache right there in the syntax.

Because they seemed to be catching on quickly, we passed out a handout with the following excerpts, which was similar to the one we'd used for sentence fragments; and without any further modeling, we asked them to do what they had done the other day: discuss with their group what they thought each author gained by writing an extremely long sentence.

And away went the two boats for the north end of the pond, while the sea-gulls wheeled and cried overhead and the taxicabs tooted and honked from Seventy-second Street and the west wind (which had come halfway across America to get to Central Park) sang and whistled in the rigging and blew spray across the decks, stinging Stuart's cheeks with tiny fragments of flying peanut shell tossed up from the foamy deep.

— E. B. WHITE, *Stuart Little* ([1945] 1973, 38)

To take off in an F-100 at dawn and cut in the afterburner and hurtle twenty-five thousand feet up into the sky so suddenly that you felt not like a bird but like a trajectory, yet with full control, full control of *five tons* of thrust, all of which flowed from your will and through your fingertips, with the huge engine right beneath you, so close that it was as if you were riding it bareback, until you leveled out and went supersonic, an event registered on earth by a tremendous cracking boom that shook windows, but up here only by the fact that you now felt utterly free of the earth—to describe it, even to wife, child, near ones and dear ones, seemed impossible.

— TOM WOLFE, *The Right Stuff* (1979, 30)

The rain was changing its nature, getting heavy turning hard, and Warren sitting cross-legged on top of a bureau felt the sting of ice, like steel pellets. He held out his hand and received a particle of hail. He put up his denim collar. He was facing forward but for some reason swiveled on his rump and looked back at the street just as the wagon behind picked up the pace to fill in the slack in the parade and it was she in her dress of tulips faded sitting up on her wagon on a stool like a princess borne in a palanquin, her body moving forward and back, her head moving in the lag of her body's rhythm and he smiled and raised his hand and she smiled and raised hers, and they stared at each other, their bodies gently bending and straightening in the rhythm of the mules' pace, the wheels creaking in the mud, the traces rattling like ancient music of fanfares and the two of them staring at each other like royal lovers in a procession toward their investiture under the hardening rain through the canyon of slag going down to the plains.

— E. L. DOCTOROW, *Loon Lake* (1982, 40)

The students quickly plunged into their groups and started talking with much animation, familiar now with both the small-group structure and the work they were expected to do. And the conversations they had did not disappoint us. Because we'd drawn their attention to connections between what a writer is trying to say and how he uses conventions to capture that, they were able to say that the E. B. White sentence captured the liveliness of Central Park and the exhilaration Stuart Little must have felt as he sailed across the boat pond (something they knew about from the movie, if not the actual book). The Tom Wolfe sentence also spoke to exhilaration and energy, power, and speed. The sentence is like a rocket, surging through the stratosphere and pushing itself beyond conventional barriers, as if it, too, were supersonic, hurtling us across the page. And the fact that he says it was impossible to describe seemed to justify, in a way, the use of so many words. The Doctorow piece seemed harder, mostly because of the vocabulary and what the passage describes, since the students were much more familiar with Central Park and rockets than they were with Western mule trains. But they caught the slow, plodding feel of the sentence that mimicked the pace of the mules and the way that the phrases seemed to sway back and forth, like the boy and girl perched in the wagons.

From this discussion, we were able to make some generalizations about why we thought writers would write wordy sentences, which again we charted as a class so the students could refer to them when they were actually writing. On the chart we noted the following:

- Writers use long, wordy sentences to capture a feeling or mood, like longing or exhilaration.
- Writers use long, wordy sentences to capture the speed of an action they're describing, whether it's fast or slow.

We then let them loose to try their hand at wordy sentences, and while we still felt some apprehension about how their growing awareness of grammar would filter down into their own writing, we were convinced from the classroom discussions that, as readers at least, their awareness and sensitivity to the power of grammar had been raised, which was our ultimate goal. Now we would see how that translated into writing.

Assessing the Assessment: A Look at Final Projects

For two weeks the students worked on their anthologies, developing pieces that tried to incorporate the different grammatical choices we'd seen writers make throughout the previous weeks. They wrote sentence fragments that acted like snapshots by isolating images. They tried on punctuation marks like hats to see which ones fit and were the best suited for the look they were trying to achieve. And they wrote long, sinuous, serpentine sentences that captured different emotions, weaving their way through phrases and clauses as they never had before. And while they wrote we conferred with them, asking them what their intentions were and sharing how we, as readers, reacted, helping them as they deliberated on choices about sentence length and punctuation. Frequently, too, we directed them back to the mentor texts, suggesting that they keep them next to them, right there on their desks, as they wrote. Many students, for instance, wrote two-word fragments, such as one student did here: *I really hate sitting in the cafeteria. All of the noise hurts my ears. The people. The food. I feel sick already.* Returning to the mentor texts to study them more closely enabled him to see that the mentor fragments were much more specific and detailed, which then inspired him to change *The food* to *The heaps of sloppy Joe's on plates. The sickening smell of ketchup.*

Almost all the students tried their hand at fragments, though some like Naomi, attempted to weave almost every effect we had talked about into one of their pieces:

> As soon as I pulled the door closed, I heard the click of its lock. I realized there was no escaping. The key turned, the car rolled out of the garage. The sky was gray. Beads of rain washed down the sides of the windows. My grandmother sat in the front: on the passenger side, right next to my dad, who was driving. My mom was next to me; we sat in the back. I could hear my grandma

talking about someone that died, or some doctor she's seen, or something she ate, or someone her friend's friend knew, or someplace she went the other day. It didn't matter what she was saying. Even if I were listening I wouldn't know any of the people or places or things she was talking about. I blocked out her voice by diving into a book. Bad idea. I got a headache. It must have been from the smell of the car, mixed with all the cologne. My gum also had something to do with it. Mint. The words on the page in front of me contributed to my headache as well. I would have opened the window if it weren't for the rain that was now pounding the windshield. I looked at my watch. 9:30 am. I bet myself we would arrive in D.C. at around 12:45—just in time for my cousin Celia's first birthday. I looked at the big, white, rectangular box directly behind my seat. Just an hour ago I had brought the cake to life. Little pink flowers. Bright red lettering: Happy 1st Birthday Celia. I leaned back into my seat . . . 10, 9, 8. I rested my head against the window . . . 7, 6, 5, 4. My eyes started to droop . . . 3, 2, 1 . . .

I awoke to the sound of waves crashing against the side of the car no it wasn't a car it was a boat a great big boat and the gray I had seen just moments before vanished without a trace and light hit here and there the brightest lights I had ever seen only they weren't lights they were colors magnificent brilliant colors I had to shade my eyes from all the things going on around me as the colors swirled into patterns and circles of all the reds blues greens yellows oranges pinks purples imaginable my skin glowed a deep amber with teal tinges and lemon undertones it's incredible I said in a whisper

   "It's incredible," I whispered.
   I came back and the car was still a car. I looked outside. It was still gray. Gray grayness everywhere. Even the grass was gray. My grandma offered me a cookie. A chocolate covered wafer. My favorite. I looked at the clock. 9:45 am. We still had a long way to go.

We see Naomi here employing different techniques to achieve a variety of effects: the long, wordy sentence with its string of *ors* that seems to capture the droning of her grandma and the boredom that the droning induces; the details of the birthday cake highlighted in fragments; and that single word *mint* set off by itself in a way that seems to release its scent, so that we stop and smell it. And the fluid, disorienting world of the dream: she abandons all punctuation there to capture that dreamy state, then signals to us that we're back in reality by resuming more standard usage.

Of course, not all of her choices fully work, like the colon in the sentence that first mentions her grandmother. She seems to be using it to suggest a relationship between the grandmother and the father that is different than the one between her and her mother, who are connected more closely through a semicolon and the pronoun *we*. But the very fact that she is trying to use punctuation to establish relationships speaks to her heightened awareness of grammar. And perhaps the punctuation hints at something that Naomi might want to explore; it suggests a dynamic or hierarchy in the family that could be fleshed out and developed, something that is still hidden in the piece—and, in fact, may be at the heart of it—lying latent in the punctuation.

And here is a piece from another student, Vicky, who also tried to combine a variety of effects, including inventing hyphenated phrases like *the thousand-change girl*:

> One night that has always seemed like a dream. One everlasting effect. My grandpa is looking down at me. A dim yellow light surrounds his face. A window with white shades is off to one side while the walls, originally white, have turned beige from the faint light. The only person that I can see through my tiny dark brown eyes is my dear old grandpa. An old man with a burnt face, from the treatment he got. Dark brown puppy eyes—sad, very sad. A glistening-tear-down-your cheek kind of sad. Smooth hair and very black. Black and slicked straight back. The ears stick out. Ears just like a little boy, little-cute-boy ears. He smiles. I hear myself laugh. I'm a tiny baby just being held by her loving grandfather—her loving grandfather who will soon pass away. I blink shut, I blink open: he's still here! I laugh again and again and I know I am still smiling. Just by looking at him, I know how much I love my grandpa. The yellow light around us darkens a bit but his face is still clear. I see him—I laugh and smile to see him.

In the reflective writing that accompanied the piece, Vicky had much to say about her choices. On her use of fragments, for instance, she wrote: "I was trying to develop a steady pace, create a distinct voice, introduce part of an idea/emotion, make the writing seem more poetic and, lastly, be simple. The main point of using the fragments was to emphasize that I was a baby. The piece is written like a baby in incomplete sentences and ideas. If the piece is simple, then the reader can think as simply as a baby would." She also consciously chose to write the piece in the present tense because, she said, "the present tense gives off a childlike voice. It also has a more-in-the-moment feel to it and shows more emotion." And as for the ending, she had this to say: "I tried to emphasize my feelings of joy at the end by writing 'I laugh and smile to see him' after the dash. By setting the laughing and smiling off with a dash, it not only gives the feeling of joy but also the sense of innocence. That's what I was really trying to go for—innocence. I was trying to go for the theme of innocence because that's how I felt. I felt very young and innocent because I was so unaware of the world." And unaware, we might add, of the specter of death, which, despite being set aside, as if quarantined, by dashes, still haunts and hovers over the piece.

We could debate how successful Vicky's been at achieving her desired effects, though given that we've already acknowledged how proficient execution often lags behind intentions, we applaud her for what she's tried to do and are pleased that she had a vision. Her reflective piece also marks a shift in what she sees as a writer's true job. It is not simply to report on what happened, as in "I did this; I did that," but to render experience and sensation so fully that a reader feels it, too, using all the grammatical tools and tricks a writer has up her sleeve. And we're pleased as well to see traces of our instruction in the reflective piece itself—in its hyphenated *more-in-the-moment feel* and the dash that sets off the word *innocence*. We take that as proof that Vicky is transferring lessons learned in one piece to another, which is a sign of independence, internalization, and retention.

But, perhaps most of all, we were pleased by the diversity of voices in the pieces. The students all wrote with rich, vibrant voices that we hadn't always seen or heard before, displaying a freshness and attentiveness to language, a relish for punctuation and words, that seemed significantly new. Here, for instance, is another excerpt from a piece by Colleen that, perhaps not coincidentally, takes as its subject the same mind-numbing feeling surrounding classrooms that Dan's piece did:

> Unfortunately, I have summer school this vacation—me and my failing grades. These are consequences; these are the results. Being stuck in a room where the amount of gravity exceeds the amount of air. Where the thermometer is about to explode. Yet there is no air conditioning—President's tight budget cuts, so sad. Sweat drops roll down the side of my face. The thick fabric of my t-shirt hugs my skin. Should have put on a tank top this morning. The classroom feels like an oven baking at 10,000 degrees. Gravitational forces pull at

my eyelids . . . weighing them down . . . nearly shut. The teacher walks over to my desk. Smacks the wooden surface with a rule. I jump up in reaction. She glares. Burning holes through my head. I look down, say sorry. She walks away and continues her lesson. Talking and more talking. Directly from the textbook. Blah blah. Blah blah blah blah. It never teaches me anything. My head doesn't absorb it. Her useless words—they swim around my head. Making me feel dizzy. I watch her mouth moving. Opening and closing. Long words leaking out of the o-shape, like beans spilling from a sack. I drag my eyes upward to the clock directly above her head. The second-hand inches one millimeter for every second. Working its way around the circle to its finishing point and starting all over at sixty seconds. The hand continues running . . . second after second . . . minute after minute. Tick tock, tick tock. Hypnotizing me with its monotonous function.

Compare the monotony the piece alludes to with the vitality of the telling and you see what can happen when students are engaged, really engaged with language. But for now we'll leave Colleen and her classmates behind, hopeful that she finds the room that spawned this writing more inspiring than the one she describes, to see what else students are able to accomplish through the practice of more focused apprenticeship.

The Sentence and the Apprentice

5

> Push it. Examine all things intensely and relentlessly. Probe and search each object in a piece of art. Do not love it, do not course over it, as if it were understood, but instead follow it down until you see it in the mystery of its own specificity and strength.
>
> — ANNIE DILLARD

The placement of a punctuation mark achieves more, sometimes, than clarity. Indeed, what is achieved is sometimes the opposite, it is ambiguity. There is surprise in punctuation, and complexity. Punctuation raises questions it does not always answer, leading the reader on, seducing. What does it mean, we wonder, when we come upon this sentence in E. B. White's *Stuart Little* ([1945] 1973, 2): "Before he was many days old he was not only looking like a mouse but acting like one, too—wearing a gray hat and carrying a small cane"? Does this truly mean, as the dash seems to suggest, that mice generally wear hats and carry canes? Is this knowledge that we are supposed to share? Or is this book, is this sentence, the start of a seduction, one that brings us a whole world that we had somehow missed—a world of mice with waistcoats and canes scurrying under our feet? There is a kind of gleeful, complicit quality to the part of the sentence that comes after the dash. The dash creates disequilibrium; it is a rocky raft carrying the reader into an unknown sea.

There is ecstasy and heartbreak in punctuation as well, as we earlier saw. There are words under the words. In *Sweet Days of Discipline*, Fleur Jaeggy's (1989) haunting novel about adolescent desire at a boarding school in Switzerland, we come upon the following passage on page 2.

It happened one day at lunch. We had all sat down. A girl arrived, a new one. She was fifteen, she had hair straight and shiny as blades and stern staring shadowy eyes . . . She spoke to no-one. Her looks were those of an idol, disdainful. Perhaps that was why I wanted to conquer her. She had no humanity. She even seemed repulsed by us all. The first thing I thought was: she had been further than I.

How suggestive and mysterious is the colon in the last sentence. It is in that colon that we experience the sudden recognition one adolescent feels for another and the sense of separateness as well. In that colon lies a glimpse of ambiguous sexual knowledge that comes to fruition with its attachment: "she had been further than I." Further how? How jagged and raw is the voice achieved by longer and shorter sentences rubbing up against each other. How sensual, really, the punctuation is, and yet awkward and stiff as well. How appropriately complex for hidden adolescent desire at a Swiss boarding school.

Lovers of punctuation notice its presence the way you always notice a beloved. We detect it. We wonder about it. We praise it. We try to enclose it. It's the way Helen, in Cathleen Schine's novel *The Love Letter*, reads through the secret and saved letters of writers and their lovers:

> She opened the other collection and read a letter from Edith Wharton to her lover, W. Morton Fullerton. "There would have been the making of an accomplished flirt in me, because my lucidity shows me each move of the game—but that, in the same instant, a reaction of contempt makes me sweep all the counters off the board & cry out:—'Take them all—I don't want to win—I want to lose everything to you!' "
> Nice punctuation, Helen thought. (1995, 120)

Nice is one way to describe Wharton's wild dashes. Desperate, daring, erotically charged would be another. Helen is afraid to surrender to this eroticism. She resists that punctuation as, in the novel, she resists the illicit pull of desire she feels for someone else. When we engage with punctuation this way, we engage at many levels, and all is not as it seems at first.

When we engage with grammar as art, we allow ourselves to wonder, surrender, be tempted and overcome. In *The Sound on the Page*, Ben Yagoda writes that "it is frequently the case that writers entertain, move and inspire us less by what they say than by how they say it" (2004, xi). Some writers put words and punctuation together in ways that unsettle, provoke, inspire, and, implicitly, teach. We may never have thought to put words and marks together as E. B. White, Sandra Cisneros, William Steig, and Vladimir Nabokov do, but once we see their effect, we can emulate them.

It is lovely to write with and for students, but we don't want our own techniques and style to become the summit of what students experience. There is more. And so we lead students through the stages of apprenticeship, teaching them to seek out mentor texts, to read them closely, and to ask: What is this writer doing that I can try in my own writing? In writing workshop, we have for many years led mentor author studies and considered the style and content of authors. Students have written short pieces in the style of Walter Dean Meyers and Nikki Giovanni. They often imitated the vocabulary, setting, and kind of story these authors relate. In a Gary Soto study, for instance, students would set their stories in a place they knew as well and as intimately as Gary Soto knows Fresno; they would create characters who were culturally torn and aware of the fact that they were not like the families they saw on prime-time TV.

But it is different to pay attention to how writers write at the sentence level. This means paying attention to the order and effect of words and punctuation, to the startling and evocative ways that some writers put these together. It means that we ask students to apprentice themselves in smaller, closer ways, so that they may generate only a sentence or two, but they consider carefully the placement of every word and every mark. We generate intimacy with language.

Student Writers Apprenticing Themselves at the Sentence Level

When we started thinking about apprenticeship at the sentence level several years ago, we recalled a song called "I Love You Period" that had played long ago on MTV. Our memory of the song was fragmentary at best, but we did recall that unlike the songs in the Public Television collection *Grammar Rocks*, which are songs *about* punctuation, this song demonstrated punctuation. Interested less in the melody than in the idea of spoken punctuation, we didn't want to transcribe, imitate, or perform this MTV-aired song, but we did want to create our version of it to describe to students, and so we put together these phrases from our memories:

Do you love me? I love you. Please, please! (I want to have you.)

First we wrote the last sentence as *(I want to have you.)*, but that, while enticing, seemed overly charged for a classroom of adolescents, and so we switched from *have* to *hold*, which is seductive but not unleashed. And so we came to this:

Do you love me? I love you. Please, please! (I want to hold you.)

Creating our own spoken melody, we recited-sang this with all the punctuation spoken aloud:

Do you love me question mark? I love you period. Please, please exclamation point! (I want to hold you in parentheses.)

It's fascinating how the punctuation becomes thrilling when we say it aloud. Say *I want to hold you in parentheses* in a rather slow, low voice, and it is shocking how provocative it sounds. *In parentheses* suggests a kind of secret, seductive place unfamiliar before in the study of grammar. *I love you period* says it all—it is much more definitive than *I love you. Period.* How bold. How intimate. How forward. Let's plunge inside those parentheses. You hear the punctuation song and you long, really, for someone to seduce you with punctuation.

This caressing of punctuation struck a chord with us, and we immediately started saying punctuation aloud sometimes during our lessons, which created a difference at once in the classroom. We realized that often student readers simply blipped over the punctuation. So reading aloud, imagining intonation based on punctuation, is a useful start. Then we conducted a small classroom inquiry with this collection of sentences, because it was so wonderful the way these sentences demonstrated the forms of period, question mark, exclamation point, and also parentheses. We started our first inquiry in an eighth-grade class, one whose writing demonstrated highly creative, inconsistent, and at times entirely confusing ending punctuation or a lack thereof. We sang the song. We asked students to describe for each other what the purpose of each punctuation mark was and how it affected meaning. Some things they said:

■ The question mark was used to show the speaker had an urgent question.

- The period clearly made his claim a definitive statement.
- The exclamation point marked an emotional cry.
- The parentheses showed something special and secret, something kept inside.

Nothing particularly radical for those of us who already are at ease with punctuation. But these were students who were not using any consistent or effective ending punctuation. This was a high-poverty middle school classroom where writing workshop flourished and many children found strong voices in their writing. It was also a classroom where teachers had struggled with grammar and students had ignored it. This was the first time we heard the students say something personal about punctuation. Next, we used the sentences as a prompt. The students could write something new, or they could take an idea from their notebooks and return to it. Either way, they were to mentor themselves to the song precisely. That very first class, Yuk-tsi, a young woman who had come from a mountain village in Fujien, China, to a tenement in New York's Chinatown four years before, turned in her notebook to these sentences:

I want to go to college. I want to go to an Ivy league college.

Yuk-tsi's writing, even in her notebook, was careful. It was carefully and accurately punctuated. Unlike her peers, Yuk-tsi did in fact use ending punctuation for her sentences. Yuk-tsi's writing was accurate. But it was flat. It demonstrated little voice. Most of her small, careful sentences ended in a period. She rarely used commas, seeming unsure how to extend her sentences. Flipping through her notebook, we saw that she had some trouble making significant punctuation choices in English and that she knew she had trouble and was going to restrain her writing in order to avoid mistakes. Following the form of the mentor text, she revised her writing so that it read:

Will I ever be a college girl? I want to walk in ivy halls. Please, please! (I don't want to stay in Chinatown.)

Yuk-tsi followed the form of the mentor sentences precisely. Yuk-tsi's sentences now carry the reader through distinct stages: her questioning her future, her naming of a particular desire, and her hidden fears. The transformation of *I want to go to college* to *Will I ever be a college girl?* is vivid. Posed as a question, it invites us to share the longing and the uncertainty that fills this young woman. We see that it is not simply about *going* to college. It is about *being* a college girl. *I want to go to an ivy league college* becomes *I want to walk in ivy halls.* Familiar with the fierce turmoil of Chinatown, we contrast that with a walk in halls covered with ivy. We see the activities and identity Yuk-tsi dreams of. And it's poetic now—*ivy halls.* With her exclamation Yuk-tsi seems to call directly to the reader, showing an awareness of audience, which is part of what gives her a stronger voice now. And the parentheses here reveal secrets too, but they are fears, not dreams. Punctuation choices help Yuk-tsi extend meaning, expand her writing, say more, reveal herself through her grammatical choices. Yuk-tsi's is an apprenticeship. She would not have composed these sentences in just this way on her own, nor may she again, yet. But she was delighted with them, as were her classmates. She could see what happens when writers take risks, and she could see one way to do that. Yuk-tsi added punctuation, she varied her sentences, and in doing so she also added voice. She found herself—her unique and particular self—on the page. Her writing demonstrates the principle Ben Yagoda holds to be true in his study of writers' influence on other writers: "in due time, after all, influence will be mitigated and eventually trumped by personality" (2004, 107).

The lovely thing about having a strong student example is, the next time you organize this inquiry in the classroom, you can offer students both the original mentor text and a piece of student writing that is based on it. So when a fifth-grade classroom studied not only the mentor text but Yuk-tsi's response in their inquiry, they said the same things the eighth-grade class had said about the purpose of the punctuation—to imply a question, a statement, a plea, a secret. But looking at Yuk-tsi's apprenticeship, they said more. Articulating what happens when we try to write this way, they said:

- It helps us add more specific detail.
- It makes our voice stronger.
- It gets us to speak more from the heart.
- It makes our writing more inviting.
- It gets us to think harder about the choices we make.
- It pushes us to take risks.

Here are some fifth-grade attempts:

Jenny's notebook entry: I want to make friends. I miss my village.

Jenny's revised entry: Will I ever make a friend here? Some faces look kind. Talk to me, talk to me! (I speak some English, really.)

Shen's notebook entry: I miss the trees and the mountains. It's ugly here.

Shen's revised entry: Will I see my mountains again? I want to smell the apple trees. Please, please! (I don't want to live in Chinatown.)

Jeff's notebook entry: I didn't make the track team.

Jeff's revised entry: Will I ever make the track team? I want to be on one team. Please, please! (It's lonely on the side.)

We see these children studying both the original mentor and Yuk-tsi's work closely. We see them respecting the way Yuk-tsi learned to take risks as a writer, and we see them following closely in her footsteps, literally picking up some of her words to use them themselves, the way she picked up words from the mentor sentences. You can almost trace the movement of phrases through the different compositions. And yet each one is different. Each reveals a different internal tension.

These children, living in Chinatown and the Lower East Side, begin to take on voice as they mentor themselves to writers who have strong voices. Because the mentor text is daring, because the mentor text reveals emotion, hints at secrets long withheld, the students do the same—they are tempted and led and they follow right along to places not imagined before. And so they tell us so much more. Their writing has so much more heart. We didn't know from their writing that Jenny and Jeff are lonely. We didn't know Jenny is frustrated that people expect her to know little English. We didn't know that Shen finds Chinatown ugly, that he came from a place that was beautiful and that he finds the transition unbearable. We didn't know that Jeff hates being shoved to the side, and that he knows that sports, at least for him, are all about belonging.

These are some things that classmates said about this writing that we recorded in our notebook. One fifth grader said, "I always thought China was awful. I didn't know it was beautiful. I always thought they were glad to come here. I thought they were lucky to be here." Shen's new writing makes his classmate stop and consider him as an individual, not as one of a nameless "they." The writing, with its voice and specificity, has prompted a new degree of empathy. Another fifth grader, an athletic and popular boy, said to Jeff, "Track sucks, you know. We stand around forever in the rain and sun and then finally after like forever, we run for like twenty seconds. It's whack." There was a bit of a pause, and then this boy added, "Anyway, what do you care? You can write and stuff."

We're sure that Jeff still longs for athletic prowess. We're sure Jeff's dreams are what Chabon, in his novel *The Adventures of Kavalier and Clay*, calls "caterpillar dreams," dreams of miraculous escape, transformation, and release (2000). In this novel, Chabon puts his finger sharply on identities and how students manage them at school as they learn what identities are acceptable. Describing a boy just the age of these fifth graders, Chabon writes:

> Tommy was a little pudgy, and small for his age. He had been the target of some standard-issue cruelty over the years, but his taciturnity and his spectacularly average performance in school had earned him a certain measure of safe invisibility. (499)

We know that peer cultures can be oppressive. We know that school is a place that is more congenial for some students than for others. We know that many students long for stronger voices and different identities, and we know, as we saw in Dan's notebook in the last chapter, that students practice silence as a form of resistance. Resistance to school, to performance, to exposure. It is a small thing, therefore, that these particular students found stronger voices by apprenticing themselves to other writers. Small because it is only a few sentences. Small because it is just one experience. And it is a not-small thing too. Not-small in the way that they have learned they can expand their writing and their voices. Not-small in the approbation and wider recognition they received from peers even just for a moment. Not-small in the continual faceting of identities.

What Apprenticeship Looks Like in the Classroom

And so, often now, we offer students not only the original mentor text but student writing that sprang from it, as they envision the paths of apprenticeship more clearly this way, and they respond to the courage or spirit of other young writers as well as to the original text. This is the way this often looks in the classroom: We put the mentor text up on a chart or an overhead. If the mentor sentence is from a picture book, then we will often preface the work by reading aloud the whole picture book, asking students to read and listen as writers, paying attention not only to the story but to language and form. If the sentence we are studying comes from a novel that is too long to read aloud in class, then we often storytell the book to create a context for the sentence so it makes sense. (For instance, when we lift a sentence from *Lolita*, as we do later on, we say that this sentence comes from a story by Nabokov about a man who adores a girl in ways that men are not supposed to adore girl-children, and unlike most, this narrator fulfills this desire in dangerous ways. Here, the narrator tells us something about his childhood.) Then we turn to the sentence at hand. With each mentor text, we spend time simply reading it closely and collectively— that is our collective inquiry. Maxine Greene calls this "reflective time" (1995, 126). It ensures that, as she puts it, there is "conscious participation in a work, a going out of energy, an ability to notice what is there to be noticed in the play, the poem, the quartet," or, we might add, the sentence (125).

Then we often study how other student writers have responded to it, by putting some of their sentences up on the overhead or chart paper. We don't need to do this for every mentor text—we don't limit our study only to texts that we have already used in prior classes. But it is useful to do it once or twice. We ask students in partnerships to say what they notice as they compare the student writing with the mentor text. Often they see things we haven't seen. Then we ask students to apprentice themselves as writers, to try writing like this, holding closely to the model in front of them. Some students take a sentence or two from their notebooks as a starting place, and they revise them following the mentor text. Others come up with a new subject, sometimes writing in the form of the mentor text right away, but more often putting some words down on paper and then working to craft them so they follow the mentor text.

It is sometimes helpful to study more than one mentor text at a time, so that students may try a variety of forms, one of which may prove itself peculiarly suited to their subject. We don't worry too much, though, that this work is really an exercise. In this work, we mentor ourselves to two writers and educators whom we greatly admire, Maureen Barbieri (1995, 2002) and Georgia Heard (1989, 1998), both of whom push teachers to be authentic with their students— to think more about writing and art and less about having a format for lessons, to have faith in students' responsiveness and their poetic sensibility and faith also in our ability to lead them by unexpected paths to undiscovered places. There are many ways to achieve voice, for teachers as well as students.

And so, what follows is a study of some mentor texts and a collection of student writing in various stages of apprenticeship. We have introduced this work as a mini-unit, a two-week study in which we tried the work every day. We have also done one or two days of the work to initiate processes of inquiry and apprenticeship and then offered various mentor texts at different times during the year. Both ways were rewarding. We've found that work begun as writing exercises lingers in surprising ways. We see it in familiar sentence constructions appearing in writer's notebooks or published pieces. We see it in the way students pay closer attention to how words and punctuation look on the page and linger in the heart. We see it in the way they begin to contend and engage with grammar and language.

Close Reading of the Artful Sentence

There is an art to reading sentences closely, naming what happens in the sentence and what the sentence accomplishes. It is the art of lingering. It is the art of expectation. It is the art of the unabashed response. It is what Ben Yagoda does in *The Sound on the Page* when he says of a comma in an otherwise spare collection of short sentences by Hemingway: "It feels like a consoling arm around our shoulder" (2004, xii). We get from language what we give to it; the more we give, the more we get back. And we can learn to make our reading practices more intricate, mostly by being willing to be changed ourselves. In *Protocols of Reading*, Robert Scholes remarks:

> Our skill, our learning, our commitment to the text will determine, for each of us, the kind of experience that text provides. Learning to read books—or pictures, or films—is not just a matter of acquiring information from texts, it is a matter of learning to read and write the texts of our lives. Reading, seen this way, is not merely an academic experience but a way of accepting the fact that our lives are of limited duration and that whatever satisfaction we may achieve in life must come through the strength of our engagement with what is around us. (1989, 19)

There is no handbook on how to read this way; we simply engage with texts expecting that we will emerge from this engagement different. The art of teaching is in naming what we find out, in holding on to new ideas, new loves, and new powers. Let us take a simple but invigorating sentence to start. It is from William Steig's picture book *Brave Irene*, which tells the story of a young girl, Irene, battling a snowstorm in order to deliver a dress her mother has sewn to a beloved and distantly located duchess. The girl is steadfast, the storm is vicious. The sentences pull us through the wild storm away from safe places toward something unknown. At one point in the story, when Irene has nearly succumbed to the snow and the wind, we come to this sentence:

> Home, where she longed to be, where she and her mother could be warm together, was far behind. (1986, 13)

Reading this sentence closely with students means we engage with it: we investigate how it works and what it accomplishes. Steig is a master of sentences that set up tension between the character and the setting. In some ways his stories reside in these constructions. So here, we name that the sentence starts by naming a place, and it is a place that is special to the character. Then it reveals how that place matters to the character—what happens there. Then it shows where that special place is now. We also name that the sentence has four parts, each separated by commas, and that they follow the order and purposes just described. Here's a third grader, mentoring herself to Steig's sentence:

> *Amanda's notebook entry:* I lost my special Rabbit last year. I still miss him.

> *Amanda's revised entry:* Rabbit, who stayed with me in the dark, who never ever left me alone, got lost in the subway.

There is a significant shift in Amanda's writing as she imitates Steig. She moves from short sentences of limited impact to longer, evocative, more poetic writing. She is no longer writing just to say what happened but to convey the full scope of her grief and her deep love for Rabbit to an audience. Amanda also demonstrates Scholes's belief that "to read at all, we must read the book of ourselves in the texts in front of us" (1989, 6). Amanda follows Steig's text closely in its form and its purpose. She highlights tension; she constructs an internal story structure within her sentence just as Steig does. But she rejects the idea of place in favor of a beloved object. For Amanda, it is all about Rabbit. She shows us how to fulfill a task set by Roland Barthes: to "rewrite the text of the work within the text of our lives" (in Scholes 1989, 49).

Amanda's writing also shows what Georgia Heard calls "poetic sensibility." In fact, by moving her words to center space, Amanda turned her piece into a poem she published in class:

Rabbit,

who stayed

with me

in the dark,

who never

ever

left me

alone,

got lost

in the subway.

It may be doubtful that Amanda's writing will demonstrate this lush poetic quality every day or that it will suggest through its carefully spaced phrases and commas an implacable narrative trajectory leading us inescapably to its fulminating tragic loss. But she learns that how we arrange words matters. She knows that we can say more and say it more artistically. And she knows where to go to find a mentor for this work.

Here is another student, a fourth grader, trying on the same Steig sentence as a mentor. In her notebook, Thalia had written:

My brother woke up to blow his nose and then his nose started bleeding. It wouldn't stop for half an hour. My mom did everything she could and then my brother started crying. My mother called the ambulance and they drove us in the ambulance car to the hospital. When I got there I sat in the waiting room. I was so bored then my dad came I was so glad. He was at work. When we came back he brought me a muffin and then we were home. 30 minutes later my brother arrived I was so glad he was alright.

Like Amanda, Thalia has a subject that matters to her, one that she's written about before. Unlike Amanda, Thalia has many words. Both students could think more about audience, about how readers long for words that are put next to each other in sparkling, surprising, or poetic ways. While Amanda cares about her lost Rabbit, and Thalia cares about her brother's nosebleed, the reader comes to care only because of how they use language. Here is Thalia mentoring herself to Steig:

> Brother, who takes care of me, who plays with me, his nose started to bleed. It wouldn't stop for a half an hour. My brother started crying. His mouth was filled with blood.
>
> Mom, who loved me, who fed me, did everything she could to help my brother. My mom called the ambulance. They drove us to the hospital. When we got there I sat in the waiting room. I was so bored. I was poking my finger in the holes of the chair. A few minutes later my dad came. I was so glad. He was at work.
>
> Dad, who loves me, who pays the bills, brought me a muffin on the way home. When we got home we started to clean the house for my mom. 30 minutes later my mom and brother arrived. I was so glad. Me and my dad almost cried.

Thalia doesn't have the discipline to pay attention to all her sentences yet. But when she does, her sentences have rhythm. She achieves some of Steig's innate sense of poetry. She puts words together in unexpected ways that make us smile. *Brother, who takes care of me, who plays with me, his nose started to bleed. Mom, who loved me, who fed me, did everything. Dad, who loves me, who pays the bills, brought me a muffin.* When we read closely, we see that Thalia has followed the Steig sentence in how she names a loved one, then describes what is special about this beloved, then says what happened. She has found what we might call a grammatical motif to unify and uplift her story, which suddenly becomes about more than a nosebleed. It's about how a family operates, how they cope and support one another. And each time she returns to the motif, she tells us a little bit more, so that in the repeated forms we begin to see different kinds of familial love.

Reading for Purpose and Tone

Some mentor sentences merit a kind of intimate engagement that we name as something beyond close reading—it is a kind of surrender to something that we cannot fully articulate, because any attempt to use language other than that of the original text reduces its metaphoric substance. In Chapter 2, for instance, we briefly looked at this excerpt from Nabokov's *Lolita* (1989, 10):

> My very photogenic mother died in a freak accident (picnic, lightning) when
> I was three.

Billy Collins writes, in *Picnic, Lightning*: "It is possible to be struck by a meteor / or a single-engine plane / while reading in a chair at home" (1998, 24). He notes, too, that Nabokov's message "can be delivered from within." We feel Nabokov's words inside us. They take up solid places, perhaps because they are nouns. And there they radiate. First there was a picnic, then there was lightning. The world is a place of great complexity. Human existence is small and easily swept away. *(Picnic, lightning)* becomes a metaphor for uncertainty, for death, for the parenthetical anguish of the everyday transactions of the world we suffer. Perhaps that is why we squirm when we read Nabokov's sentence. It makes us uneasily aware of what Scholes said: "that our lives are of limited duration."

And yet there is delight, too, in reading Nabokov. There is pleasure to be found in the almost flip tone, in the way he notes and sets aside happenings that would feel monumental elsewhere. We can try to analyze the sentence. *My very photogenic mother* names someone who is close to the narrator. The words also give a sense of someone whom the narrator knows only through photographs and memories, and the tone is rather distant, not particularly loving. *Died in a freak accident* tells what happened to this person, again in that rather dry, distant tone. *(Picnic, lightning)* alludes to a pastoral-horrific narrative, a story that is both told and not told by these two nouns put together, these nouns that create images in our head. *When I was three* lets us know how long ago this was and that it is a story perhaps remembered only through story. *My very photogenic mother died in a freak accident (picnic, lightning) when I was three.* There is an almost sarcastic voice that emerges from the order and choice of the words, a detached tone of someone who observes unpleasant happenings but is able to retain some distance from them.

It is often helpful to actually chart sentences, describing the effect of every part. It is like the old-fashioned diagrams, only instead of diagramming parts of speech, we are parsing for meaning. For these sentences, for instance, it looks like this:

Home, where she longed to be, where she and her mother could be warm together, was far behind.

place or object | how narrator feels about it | what happens when they're together | where it is now

My very photogenic mother | died in a freak accident | (picnic, lightning) | when I was three.

describes someone and relation to narrator | tells what happened | gives secret story in images | tells when it was

Then we look at the parts of speech also, because it matters that Steig's sentence starts with a noun and that the words inside Nabokov's parentheses are two nouns. We still avoid technical terms as much as possible, relying on our study, described in Chapter 3, of subject, predicate, and how writers extend these parts of the sentence:

Home, where she longed to be, where she and her mother could be warm together, was far behind.

noun (subject) | parenthetic expression | parenthetic expression | verb phrase (predicate)

My very photogenic mother | died in a freak accident | (picnic, lightning) | when I was three.

pronoun adverb adjective noun (subject) | verb phrase (predicate) | (noun, noun) | prepositional phrase

We see Jenny paying attention to this kind of parsing for meaning, as well as the parts of speech, when she revises her original notebook entry:

My mother couldn't keep me when I was twelve.

Jenny's first revision looked like this:

My mother felt unable to keep me (on welfare, living in projects) when I was twelve.

In a peer conference with her writing response group (four students who read each other's writing often), Jenny listened to her peers, who said that she could still make her own writing closer to the mentor sentence. Efram noticed that what was inside Nabokov's parentheses were nouns and only nouns. "You don't need all that other stuff," he said. Jenny revised again, to come to this:

My mother felt unable to keep me (welfare, the projects) when I was twelve.

Efram, again, noted that Jenny had work to do. "What kind of mother?" he asked. Jenny revised again:

My not so loving mother felt unable to keep me (welfare, the projects) when I was twelve.

"You're only supposed to have one adjective," said Efram. Jenny's group called their teacher over and learned that some writers hyphenate words to make a single descriptive. Jenny adopted that form. She made another decision on her own. Running Nabokov's words over her tongue, saying them aloud, she considered the rhythm, the pace of his sentence. At their table, the students noticed the way the beginning of the sentence rolls off softly and easily, until it gets to *freak* and then the *k* makes a sharp insertion, a kind of jagged note in the sentence, from which it takes the rest of the sentence to recover. There is a kind of internal story tension in the sentence. Jenny said her sentence aloud, again and again, and she decided to move her parentheses, so that we wouldn't get to *keep*, which for her was the moment of story crisis, until after we had heard about *(welfare, the projects)*. And so her final sentence reads:

My not-so-loving mother felt unable (welfare, the projects) to keep me when I was twelve.

Our hearts turn over, now, when we read Jenny's sentence. The sentiment inside this student is the same as it was when she first wrote, but now she has a poetic form that matches her sentiment. She has composed the book of herself in the text in front of her, and in doing so she has reached an audience far greater than before, readers who can feel her anguish and pain even if they have never met her.

It is a complicated sentence. It evokes empathy for the narrator, pain for all involved, and because of the careful placement of words, surprising sympathy for this mother, too. It suggests a vision of urban poverty, of adolescent experience, that is almost unbearable. Mark Currie, when describing narrative theory, says that "the only way to explain who we are is to tell our own story, to select key events which characterize us and organize them according to the formal principles of narrative" (1998, 17). This sentence is Jenny's story. It introduces characters, setting as both physical and emotional space, tension between these, and consequences. The style is like Nabokov, and yet unlike it in effect because he writes fiction and she is writing memoir. And because Jenny is an eighth grader, even as she imitates Nabokov's detachment, that very detachment seems transparent and full of pathos.

Reading for Rhythm

Jenny achieves voice. Voice is such a complicated, elusive thing. It is perhaps the matching of form and content. It is perhaps the emergence of subjects of deep personal concern. It is perhaps the tone we sense at the heart of the piece, what we might call the essence of the person who is the writer. Yet sometimes voice reflects collaborative efforts. Its rhythms and sounds and concerns may embody the experience of more than one. We learned this as we witnessed a group of students collectively composing a voice. The whole group participated, but it was from Efram that we especially learned this. Efram, a young, black, male middle school student, who had been held back once, who only reluctantly wrote in school, was a private composer of rap songs. He could compose with complicated rhyme schemes. Often his songs followed formal patterns from which they would then break out, surprising the audience. As a songwriter, Efram showed a finely nuanced sense of craft, purpose, and audience.

Efram rarely wrote in school unless someone interviewed him and transcribed for him. He was, however, an active writing partner and much sought out in peer conferences. His ability to hold a whole story in his head, and remember individual phrases and sentences, was remarkable. His face would light up when he heard words put together in ways that pleased him. One day, when we were studying mentor sentences, we looked at this one by William Steig. It is from *Amos and Boris*, a picture book about a young mouse named Amos, who, eager for adventure, sets sail on a boat that he builds himself:

> One night, in a phosphorescent sea, he marveled at the sight of some whales spouting luminous water; and later, lying on the deck of his boat gazing at

the immense, starry sky, the tiny mouse Amos, a little speck of a living thing in the vast living universe, felt thoroughly akin to it all. (1971, 7)

Efram loved this sentence, as did we all. We loved the way it made music and images as it came off the tongue and into our ears. We loved the way it told so much about Amos and his way of seeing the world as magical, full of beauty and possibility. We loved the sparkling words. *Phosphorescent, luminous, vast.* We parsed it for meaning, and our diagram looked like this:

the time | where the narrator is | what the narrator sees | time passing | what the narrator does next | how the narrator compares with his environment | how the narrator feels about this environment

In this study, students were choosing among a variety of mentor sentences to practice apprenticeship. Rameeka was in a writing response group with Efram. She brought out a notebook entry that she had written earlier in the year. It was 2001, and the school was a small school only blocks from the World Trade Center. The school had been evacuated on September 11. When school reopened, the block was often gray with smoke, and flakes of black grit lodged in your eyes, and the air smelled of unthinkable things smoldering. The buildings kept burning and burning for weeks and then months. Children had nosebleeds, teachers had migraines and sore throats. Men with machine guns patrolled the street and the entrance to the school. Many children searched for words to describe the complexity of the experience. Rameeka's notebook entry said:

One day when I came to school the buildings burst into fire and we were so scared and we all had to evacuate. Then I was so scared because we had to come back, and there was still smoke, and even fires. Everyone in my class is still scared.

Like Amanda and Thalia, Rameeka has a meaningful subject, and like those others, we care about her subject because we care about her. We know that it's an experience that is deeply personal. Her writing, however, doesn't match the power of her feelings. We are sympathetic. We share knowledge of this experience, and we empathize. But there is nothing about Rameeka's words that particularly moves. We can want and expect children to be better writers. We can tell them that we want our hearts to turn over when we read their writing. We want to hear music, we want to see pictures, we want their writing to give us visions. So far, what Rameeka has is a subject. We can tell her that there is great potential for beauty in her words and that she is a writer, now, looking for form.

In conference with her peer writing response group, Rameeka decided to revise her entry using Steig as a mentor text, because like Steig, she too was telling about something a narrator saw. Rameeka first reordered her phrases to mirror Steig's. As she reordered, she also imitated Steig's punctuation:

> One day, when I came to school, the buildings burst into fire and we all had to evacuate; and later, seeing the smoke and fires, the seventh grade was scared to come back.

Just by reordering her phrases, and by tucking them all into one long sentence, Rameeka accomplishes a more poetic rhythm. She also begins to create a sense of story tension. First something happens, then something else. We see consequences. In her original notebook entry, Rameeka simply told what happened, without any attempt to build tension, to pace it out. What is interesting, though, is the way Efram now intervened.

Efram said, "You have to count the syllables." What he meant was, to truly mentor ourselves as writers to this text, we had to reproduce the syllabic count. Efram's musicality demanded apprenticeship at this level. We had spoken as a class about words that sparkle, and how punctuation can enhance their power, but until Efram brought it up, we hadn't spoken about syllabic count (although now we always do). Rameeka wasn't willing to always submit to syllabic parallelism, but she opened up to how it would lead to a search for more lively words. With Efram's help, she contended with it. Steig's phrase *in a phosphorescent sea* has seven syllables. Rameeka's phrase *when I came to school* first became *under a blue sky* to match the description of setting more closely. Then Efram and Rameeka worked on the syllabic count. Counting *sparkling* as three syllables (*spar-k-ling*), which Efram insisted on, noting that only people with no ear for sound would think the *k* was not its own syllable, Rameeka's table came up with *in a sparkling blue sky*, which also has seven syllables. It was the same urge to extend the syllabic count that would change *city* to *metropolis* in

Rameeka's final version, a change that reflected a collaborative search for longer, livelier words and Efram's syllabic counseling. The final text, which is really a collective one, reads:

> One morning, in a sparkling blue sky, we watched the buildings shoot gray smoke over the city; and later, coming back to our little school breathing in the gritty, smelly smoke, our class, just a small seventh grade in this dark metropolis, felt entirely lost and alone.

It is poetry and music. It is Steig's form, but it is not Steig's mouse. It is a small seventh grade in a dark metropolis. It follows the form of Steig's sentence, but it accomplishes effects that are not the same. Amos watches whales spout luminous water. Rameeka and her peers watch buildings shoot gray smoke. It's the same syntactical pattern. Noun verb adjective noun. It works—the sentence tells a story and evokes a mood. Steig tells what happens to Amos and he tells how he feels about the world, and he feels kinship. Rameeka and her peers tell what happens and how they feel, and they feel entirely lost and alone. Perhaps it is the move from fiction to nonfiction, perhaps it is the move from a magical story line to story lines students don't want to inhabit. Perhaps it is the tension between these spaces that makes their work compelling. For these students compose now, not as seventh graders alone, but as seventh graders who have collectively read and absorbed another writer's music.

The List Sentence

Sometimes what we see in these compelling sentences is that the writer is using an ordinary form but paying extraordinary attention to it. Many writers, for instance, employ lists in their sentences and in their stories. Some writers, however, make of these lists something joyful. Here is William Steig's description, also from *Amos and Boris*, of Amos loading his boat with the supplies he envisions he will need for this uncharted journey:

> When the boat was finished, he loaded it with cheese, biscuits, acorns, honey, wheat germ, two barrels of fresh water, a compass, a sextant, a telescope, a saw, a hammer and nails and some wood in case repairs should be necessary,

a needle and thread for the mending of torn sails, and various other necessities such as bandages and iodine, a yo-yo and playing cards. (1971, 3)

First he tells us when this happens, then he tells us all the things that will go in the boat, and they seem to appear in order of importance. Within the list, objects are grouped with particular care, so that the hammer and saw and wood come together, and we find an explanation for their use. Same with the needle and thread. Then at the end, almost as an afterthought, come the other things that end up forgotten in our pockets or at the bottom of boats.

Lists are a useful structure. We see lists in poetry, in narratives, in essays, in journalism. It is worth experimenting with lists. And so in one fifth-grade class, as a writing exercise, we had children list what was in their backpacks. Nelson wrote:

What I have in my backpack—food, some trick toys left over from halloween, the phone my mom makes me keep, a Gameboy, and my homework.

Nelson's is a list as a list would appear if a writer did nothing in particular with it. It is just a list and barely a list. Then we studied Steig's list as a mentor text. We talked about how he named each object carefully, how he put some things together, how he told the purpose of some objects, and how there was a sense of deliberate order, until the end when it appeared a bit more haphazard and playful. We talked about how the list lets the reader envision the whole trip and all the possible happenings. We get a picture of many separate events from the objects and their potential use. We learn something about the owner as well—that the owner is someone who prepares for many eventualities. That the owner has a grand sense of which items are significant to his well-being.

Apprenticing himself to Steig, Nelson revised his list so it looked like this:

Before I zipped my backpack, I put in it some gum, raisins, peanuts, cheerios, gold fish, two juice boxes, a ball, a yo-yo, a plastic spider and a fart bag in case math was boring, a cell-phone with my mother's number on it in case I got sent to the office, and some emergency supplies such as M&M's, a Gameboy, and a copy of John's math homework.

Nelson learns to delight in his list, as Steig delights in details, in objects, in the close observation and description of the everyday world. Nelson also learns something writers know: writers fictionalize and extend in the service of art. Nelson adds two juice boxes to carefully imitate the two barrels of freshwater that Amos included. He carries a cell phone, really, because after September 11, all students and parents in this school downtown carry cell phones in case they need to find out where their families are quickly. But Nelson says something else. He avoids the large catastrophe in favor of a smaller, invented one. He introduces a voice with a sense of anarchy, of playfulness and drollness, that evokes the whimsical adventurism of Steig's text, where a little mouse sets out into the world with the personal stuff that will carry him through safely.

E. B. White is another master of the list sentence. His lists are more patrician and elegiac, evocative of a certain purity. From *Stuart Little*, here is a sentence listing what Stuart envisions as he imagines his first date:

> With his eyes shut he seemed to see the whole occasion plainly—how she would look when she came down the path to the water, how calm and peaceful the river was going to be in the twilight, how graceful the canoe would seem, drawn up on the shore. ([1945] 1973, 116)

Eighth grader Jeff was particularly intrigued with this sentence when we studied its form in class, for how it illuminated what we dream when we dream of love. It was in the weeks after the eighth-grade prom, a much heralded, feared, and discussed event at this small school. Jeff noted that E. B. White's list constructed around love an atmosphere of tranquility, beauty, and peace. It implies that the narrator has total control, at least in his dreams.

Because we know how love goes, this Arcadian reverie creates excruciating tension. Its careful world is, we know, not truly available. The dash marks the descent into fantasy, fantasy with a touch of whimsy. Jeff apprenticed himself to this text twice, writing:

> With his eyes shut he saw them plainly at the prom—how she would look up at him, how she would put her slender arms around him, how he would hold her close, dancing gracefully.

> Later he remembered it painfully—how he stabbed her with the corsage pin, how blood stained her dress, how she cried quietly, refusing to look at him.

Pained perhaps with the story, but pleased with the form, Jeff decided to add to it. He read the chapter in *Stuart Little* to find out what happened on Stuart's date. Only that chapter—Jeff wouldn't read the rest of the text because he considered it a children's book. But he read that chapter, and he considered it as a narrative of how love goes awry. Then Jeff published his piece as a poem, which he called "First Date" and dedicated to Stuart L.:

First Date: To Stuart L.

With his eyes shut
he saw them plainly
at the prom—
how she would look up at him,
how she would put her slender arms around him,
how he would hold her close,
dancing gracefully.

Later he remembered
it painfully—
how he stabbed her with the corsage pin,
how blood stained her dress,
how she cried quietly,
refusing to look at him.

With eyes now open
he knows
how it will be—
how the canoe leaks,
how the car won't start,
how the girl will leave,
always alone.

Jeff, Amanda, Jenny, and Rameeka are unafraid to make the work their own, to develop their own voices by noticing the craft of other writers. That is apprenticeship—students playing with language, noticing how writers do what they do, experimenting themselves, developing some of the habits and practices of the writers they will become.

What Makes a Mentor Sentence

When we're looking for mentor sentences, some authors' texts are particularly productive. William Steig's sentences are rhythmic, poetic, suggestive, and at the same time lucid. He shows students how to vary sentence structure and extend meaning. He shows how to say more, lavish attention on detail, suggest point of view. E. B. White's sentences are more spare, and are always entirely specific, as we see here in this one from *Stuart Little*:

> The thought of death made Stuart sad, and he began to think of his home and of his father and mother and brother and of Margalo and Snowbell and of how he loved them (all but Snowbell) and of what a pleasant place his home was, specially in the early morning with the light just coming in through the curtains and the household stirring and waking. ([1945] 1973, 61)

Roald Dahl's sentences often have that same list structure, but they are more irreverent. The voice is almost mocking. Here is one sentence from *James and the Giant Peach*:

> The Mayor of New York called up the President of the United States down in Washington, D.C., to ask him for help, and the President, who at that moment was having breakfast in his pajamas, quickly pushed away his half-eaten plate of Sugar Crisps and started pressing buttons right and left to summon his Admirals and his Generals. ([1961] 1996, 108)

Sandra Cisneros, on the other hand, often writes sentences that are lush and evocative, sentences that stagger and reel and swoon as if she were drunk on language. Take this one from *Woman Hollering Creek*, which technically is not a sentence at all, but an extended fragment:

> Lucy Anguiano, Texas girl who smells like corn, like Frito Bandito chips, like tortillas, something like that warm smell of *nixtamal* or bread the way her head smells when she's leaning close to you over a paper cut-out doll or on the porch when we are squatting over marbles trading this pretty crystal that leaves a blue star on your hand for that giant cat-eye with a grasshopper green spiral in the center like the juice of bugs on the windshield when you drive to the border, like the yellow blood of butterflies. (1991a, 3)

When we are collecting mentor sentences, we collect ones that we think are precise, poetic, or provocative. We like to gather writers who demonstrate diverse styles. We consider the structures inside the sentence. Both the E. B. White sentence and the Dahl sentence have an internal structure that is a list. We consider detail. How writers pay attention to detail often reveals the voice. That Stuart loved them (all but Snowbell) tells us that this is not a purely sentimental voice. That the President was eating Sugar Crisps tells us this is an impudent voice, one skeptical of grown-up authority. We look for action in the sentence, for how the sentence moves the story along or tells a small story itself. We read the sentence aloud and we listen for lilting rhythm and for what interrupts the rhythm. We consider the word choice. We consider the punctuation and how it ushers us through the sentence.

Sometimes, we have found mentor sentences in stories we are reading aloud in class or to our own children. Other times it is our love of certain sentences that dictates some of what we choose to read aloud. Sometimes students pass things on to us. Secondary students read William Steig and Roald Dahl and E. B. White with great relish when they are reading as writers, which is a way to enjoy a vast array of literature that might otherwise be deemed childlike. Sometimes we find sentences in the books we read for pleasure. One of the great pleasures of coming to love grammar is the way it enriches our reading.

Combining Sentences: Variation, Tone, Voice

We can also study how writers combine sentences. The patterns of a writer's sentences are often as intriguing as the patterns of word placement and punctuation within a single sentence. Dahl often leads the reader along and then brings her up short, by writing long sentences followed by short ones and fragments. Here is how he tells of the fatal crushing of Aunt Sponge and Aunt Spiker in *James and the Giant Peach*:

> They both lay on the ground, fighting and clawing and yelling and struggling frantically to get up again, but before they could do this, the mighty peach was upon them.
> There was a crunch.
> And then there was silence.
> The peach rolled on. ([1961] 1996, 42)

Teachers often tell students to vary their sentence structure, and indeed, even the rubrics for state standardized tests give credit (although no instructions) for doing this. However, "Vary your sentence structure" is pretty vague when it is divorced from purpose. When we look at Dahl's collection of sentences, we see why and *how* do to this. We see how it is the contrast that matters, and we see that the move from longer sentences to shorter ones creates a sudden change of pace. It is startling. First there is the complicated, messy scene, where they fight and claw and yell and struggle, and this is all told in one long, messy sentence. Then it is over. The combination of the shorter sentences and the line breaks, which we usually talk of only in poetry but here returns us to our lesson on paragraphing for dramatic effect, is tremendous.

Here is eighth grader Jeff, who had mentored himself to E. B. White, but who now looks to Roald Dahl. Jeff returns to his same prom story:

> He stood before her, sweating and silent and gripping the pin, desperately eyeing her breast, wondering how to shove the pin through the dress, and through the flower, and yet miss the soft pale skin underneath, skin that he longed, actually, to touch, but not with a sharp pin in his hand, and Jesus H. Christ what about the bra?
>
> He shoved the pin.
> She screamed.
> And bled.
> The prom rolled on.

Where before Jeff had the tight, parallel structure of E. B. White, here he has the anarchical wildness of Dahl. Where before he followed E. B. White to create a kind of epic, universal tragedy, here he follows Dahl to imply an inescapable farce. Jeff shows us that students can imitate other writers to useful effect, that style is something we can experiment with, that students can mirror other voices and still retain their own.

Jeff also shows us that it's worthwhile to work on small pieces of writing—that we can linger in vignettes and small anecdotes and learn to write these artistically before embarking on enormous narratives. Jeff holds to his unsafe story. He realizes that he has a good story here. He knows that trouble is the friend of the writer. And through apprenticeship, he is realizing that there are many ways to tell this story, that he has many possible options to explore and many ways to augment his own voice. Jeff does one more apprenticeship, mentoring himself to Nabokov to try to tell the whole story in one sentence:

> The pale and eager girl fled bleeding (corsage pin, boy) from the prom.

When Ben Yagoda analyzes style and voice in *The Sound on the Page* (2004), he ponders the question of how certain writers vary their style within each novel, and yet the reader senses a similarity across all the novels, a kind of distinctive voice that they recognize as peculiar to the author. We see this in Jeff's three variations—he tells the same story, the style differs, but a self-deprecating, dramatic-but-knowingly-so adolescent voice runs through each piece.

Verb Tense and Its Variations

Sandra Cisneros is another writer who puts sentences together in intriguing ways. Cisneros's sentences are suggestive rather than explicit. Her style is lyrical. Her sentences are long usually, and when there is a short one it grasps our attention. She shifts tense sometimes, and it is worth pausing to consider why. Here is the start of "One Holy Night," from *Woman Hollering Creek*:

> He said his name was Chaq. Chaq Uxmal Paloquin. That's what he told me. He was of an ancient line of Mayan kings. Here, he said, making a map with the heel of his boot, this is where I come from, the Yucatan, the ancient cities. This is what Bot Baby said.
>
> It's been eighteen weeks since Abuelita chased him away with the broom, and what I'm telling you I never told nobody, except Rachel and Lourdes, who know everything. He said he would love me like a revolution, like a religion. Abuelita burned the pushcart and sent me here, miles from home, in this town of dust, with one wrinkled witch woman who rubs my belly with jade, and sixteen nosy cousins.
>
> I don't know how many girls have gone bad from selling cucumbers. I know I'm not the first. My mother took the crooked walk too. I'm told, and I'm sure my Abuelita has her own story, but it's not my place to ask. (1991, 27)

In an inquiry with seventh graders, students talked first about the three short sentences that start the narrative—how those give a kind of sharp tone to the story, as if the narrator is upset. So already we are suspicious of Chaq. And within the sentences, we pay attention to the words and word order. She doesn't say *his name was Chaq*. She says: *He said his name was Chaq*. Suspicious. Then we get a longer sentence where we find out that they talked, and that he said he was from ancient kings. And all of this is in the past tense, all this talking and Chaq. And so we know, already, that Chaq is not around anymore.

Then the next paragraph, students noticed, is in present tense. It is eighteen weeks later. And when the narrator talks about Chaq, she returns to the past tense and the conditional, which is the tense writers use for things that may or may not happen. *He said he would love me like a revolution.* He is not saying it anymore. It was a *would* thing, a conditional state and it is gone now. And it is by paying attention to tense that we notice she was sent here (in the past) by Abuelita, but that now a witch woman rubs her belly with jade. In the present, Chaq is gone and her belly is swelling.

Then the final paragraph is both present tense, for what the narrator is thinking, and past tense, for when she thinks of her mother and grandmother, and in this mix she thinks that they are the same, these women past and present, they all took *the crooked walk*.

That's the start of a close reading—it means we pay attention to everything we can; we assume that stuff matters. This kind of close reading really helped the seventh graders navigate this difficult, beautiful text. They came to see, by following the tense change, that Chaq had abandoned the narrator, and that she is seemingly pregnant, and that perhaps that is how her mother and grandmother got pregnant too, by some boy talking to a girl at a pushcart. In talking about tense, the students also suggested that the change shifts the narration from a story about people in the narrator's past to a story about herself. They suggested that when she speaks in the present tense she is saying how she really feels about herself now. They suggested that the author wanted to link a sense of history, of ties to the Yucatan, of girls going bad, to a sense of the present and possibilities for her future.

Sandra Cisneros is heady material for a mentor text. But we have learned to trust that students respond intuitively to the art of language. Here is Rameeka's apprenticeship:

My mother was African-American, and my grandmother was African-American, and my great-great-great-great-great-grandmother was just African, until they came and took her away, I guess, in a ship, away from that place where her grandmother was, and her great-great-great-great-great-grandmother maybe lived in some ancient city in Africa.

And I don't know that ancient city, but if only that woman in Africa knew, her great-great-great-great-great-great granddaughter lives in a city too. Not an ancient city but a city full of African-Americans. Years passed, and passed since that boat came, but I wonder if she does know, and if she's with me here in this city, and maybe all the African-American girls I see in my city have their great-great-great-great-great-African grandmothers with them.

Rameeka follows Cisneros closely, holding to her words as a guide, so that she starts in past tense and tells us something about her history. Then she moves into present tense to give us an idea of the wonderings she has in her head as she moves through her modern city. Finally, she goes back again to recover that past and bring it into the present, gathering her ancestors with her and enfolding them into her own identity. Rameeka's idea is her own, but her craft is Cisneros-like and her story becomes a kind of sister story to the one told by the published writer. She writes in apprenticeship and in kinship with Cisneros.

The Potential of Apprenticeship

Rameeka, and Jeff, and Jenny, and the other students whose work we share here have the opportunity through apprenticeship to have many teachers of writing. They are started on a journey that they can continue without their classroom teacher. These students' writing may always be informed by the craft of diverse authors whose art is well beyond our own. And we know that their reading is richer, because we get emails sometimes, like the one from Jenny that said: "Isn't this sentence fab?" Below that was this sentence, from Jaeggy's *Sweet Days of Discipline*, a novel that Jenny introduced to us and which we have since read with pleasure:

> It seems pointless repeating that I took no interest in any of the other girls; having said which, I could, if questioned, perhaps admit that I was in love with Frederique. (1989, 42)

Below this quote, Jenny wrote another question: "Don't you love the way the semicolon turns everything around; isn't that love, really?"

Some Mentor Sentences

Do you love me? I love you. Please, please! (I want to hold you.)

My very photogenic mother died in a freak accident (picnic, lightning) when I was three.
Lolita, Nabokov 1989, 10

They both lay on the ground, fighting and clawing and yelling and struggling frantically to get up again, but before they could do this, the mighty peach was upon them.

> There was a crunch.

> And then there was silence.

> The peach rolled on.

James and the Giant Peach, Dahl [1961] 1996, 42

The Mayor of New York called up the President of the United States down in Washington, D.C., to ask him for help, and the President, who at that moment was having breakfast in his pajamas, quickly pushed away his half-eaten plate of Sugar Crisps and started pressing buttons right and left to summon his Admirals and his Generals.
James and the Giant Peach, Dahl [1961] 1996, 108

One night, in a phosphorescent sea, he marveled at the sight of some whales spouting luminous water; and later, lying on the deck of his boat gazing at the immense, starry sky, the tiny mouse Amos, a little speck of a living thing in the vast living universe, felt thoroughly akin to it all.
Amos and Boris, William Steig 1971, 3

When the boat was finished, he loaded it with cheese, biscuits, acorns, honey, wheat germ, two barrels of fresh water, a compass, a sextant, a telescope, a saw, a hammer and nails and some wood in case repairs should be necessary, a needle and thread for the mending of torn sails, and various other necessities such as bandages and iodine, a yo-yo and playing cards.
Amos and Boris, William Steig 1971, 3

Home, where she longed to be, where she and her mother could be warm together, was far behind.

Brave Irene, William Steig 1986, 13

Before he was many days old he was not only looking like a mouse but acting like one, too—wearing a gray hat and carrying a small cane.

Stuart Little, E. B. White [1945] 1973, 2

And away went the two boats for the north end of the pond, while the seagulls wheeled and cried overhead and the taxicabs tooted and honked from Seventy-second Street and the west wind (which had come halfway across America to get to Central Park) sang and whistled in the rigging and blew spray across the decks, stinging Stuart's cheeks with tiny fragments of flying peanut shell tossed up from the foamy deep.

Stuart Little, E. B. White [1945] 1973, 38

The thought of death made Stuart sad, and he began to think of his home and of his father and mother and brother and of Margalo and Snowbell and of how he loved them (all but Snowbell) and of what a pleasant place his home was, specially in the early morning with the light just coming in through the curtains and the household stirring and waking.

Stuart Little, E. B. White [1945] 1973, 61

In the loveliest town of all, where the houses were white and high and the elm trees were green and higher than the houses, where the front yards were wide and pleasant and the back yards were bushy and worth finding out about, where the streets sloped down to the stream and the stream flowed quietly under the bridge, where the lawns ended in orchards and the orchards ended in fields and the fields ended in pastures and the pastures climbed the hill and disappeared over the top toward the wonderful wide sky, in this loveliest of all towns Stuart stopped to get a drink of sarsaparilla.

Stuart Little, E. B. White [1945] 1973, 100

With his eyes shut he seemed to see the whole occasion plainly—how she would look when she came down the path to the water, how calm and peaceful the river was going to be in the twilight, how graceful the canoe would seem, drawn up on the shore.

Stuart Little, E. B. White [1945] 1973, 116

It happened one day at lunch. We had all sat down. A girl arrived, a new one. She was fifteen, she had hair straight and shiny as blades and stern staring shadowy eyes . . . Her looks were those of an idol, disdainful. Perhaps that was why I wanted to conquer her. She had no humanity. She even seemed repulsed by us all. The first thing I thought was: she had been further than I.

Sweet Days of Discipline, Fleur Jaeggy 1989, 2

Clearly I wasn't as elegant as she was. She wore grey skirts, loose blouses, grey, dark-blue, or powder-blue pullovers, all loose. I had a lot of tight pullovers and wide skirts with very tight waists. I pulled the waist as tight as possible with broad belts, as almost everyone else did. And that is not elegance.

Sweet Days of Discipline, Fleur Jaeggy 1989, 18

It seems pointless repeating that I took no interest in any of the other girls; having said which, I could, if questioned, perhaps admit that I was in love with Frederique.

Sweet Days of Discipline, Fleur Jaeggy 1989, 42

Afterword

I have always been fond of books that have little quotations at the head of each chapter.

— GERTRUDE STEIN

Like Gertrude Stein, we care for quotations. We love them for the chunk of wisdom they pack into a single sentence and for the way they inspire and teach us and reaffirm our beliefs. They can be like beacons, shedding light on a world that too often is dark and confusing, or like compasses that help us gain our bearings and point us in the right direction. And so as a parting bequest, we offer two more here as guides. The first is by way of André Gide, who offers this reminder: "One does not discover new lands without consenting to lose sight of the shore for a very long time." And the second is from Emerson, who says, "What lies behind us and what lies before us are tiny matters compared to what lies within."

We attest to how often we felt lost at sea as we struggled with the problems and challenges that grammar instruction presents. We questioned our thinking again and again, debated, discussed, and argued—and tried out more lessons and approaches than we hint at here. That's the work of teaching, and it is ongoing work. So while we now have some answers and approaches, we know that there is still work to do. And there is work to do not only with students but with educators. There is work to do in acknowledging racism and the cultural inflections of language codes. There is work to do in making power more visible and in considering ways to alter a status quo in schooling that privileges some students and alienates others. There is work to do in considering part of the responsibility of teaching as the labor of paying close attention to language and to literature. Contemporary writers are shifting the norms of language all the time. Contemporary researchers are reconceptualizing the complex relationships of school, curricula, and adolescent identity construction. And so none of us can ever rest on what we have already learned. Always, we look outward. This outward-looking quality of the educator is what leads to the possibility of change, in ways that seem small and ways that seem grand, in ways that are personal and ways that come to be collective or institutional.

We see, for instance, spaces in this work that are not yet illuminated. And so we consider what we will bring forward with us in our work—the current knowledge we have of implementing collaborative inquiry, the latent possibility of apprenticeship in productive texts, the possibility of explanation through direct instruction. We bring forward a concern with how grammatical choices affect meaning, voice, and power. And yet we remain open to the possibility that our understanding of grammar itself will shift.

One such space that we are interested in exploring is that of subject-verb agreement. We remain interested in ways to teach subject-verb agreement that will provide students with an incentive and motivation to take that work on. We think the key to this is point of view—that writers make sure that their verbs match their subjects because they are deeply invested and choosy about who is telling the story. They deliberate between first person and third, and even occasionally second, because they know how much that choice matters. Each point of view creates different effects; each has its attractions and drawbacks. First person, for example, creates intimacy. The writer or narrator speaks to the reader one-on-one, in confidence, though in exchange for that intimate window, the reader is barred from entering another person's or character's mind. Third person provides a wider scope and access; it has authority, but it comes with distance. And second person has an intrigue and complicity all of its own, propelling the reader into essays and stories with all the force of an imperative.

If we invited students to explore the power inherent in point of view, we imagine that students would attend to verb agreement just as we've seen them attend to tense endings when they see how much the choice of tense matters and they understand tense's effects. We can envision designing an inquiry into point of view where students would read a range of texts and think about the effects and impact of the writer's point-of-view choice. They could think about what doors were opened with that choice and, conversely, what doors were closed, gaining an appreciation as they did of the possibilities and limitations of each. Or they, and we, might find out other things.

We imagine that teachers and students could collaborate in searching out mentor texts. Classrooms and libraries abound with texts written in first and third person, but we want to choose carefully, picking passages from texts that speak to literature's highest aims—what Annie Dillard rhetorically addresses when she asks, "Why are we reading, if not in the hope of beauty laid bare, life heightened and its deepest mysteries probed?" (1989, 72). And so we might choose a first-person text, like this excerpt from *Jazmin's Notebook*, by Nikki Grimes:

> It seems to me that ideas are like gossamer, or mist, fragile as a dream forgotten as soon as you awake. I guess that's why they're so hard to hold on to. But that's also what makes them wonderful, and more than worth all the trouble.
>
> I was in Central Park last Saturday when the idea of a poem sprinkled down on me, like a sudden shower, and I knew it wouldn't last long.
>
> I grabbed a pencil from behind my ear. I'd stuck it there that morning when I'd done homework, and boy was I glad. Panic set in, though, when I checked my pockets for paper. Wallet and keys were all I had on me because I'd gotten the notion from a kid at school that traveling light was cool.
>
> *No problem*, I told myself, and went up to the first stranger I could find to beg for a notebook page, or a napkin, or even a piece of tissue. But as soon as the lady saw me approach, she waved me away. Another woman told me, flatly, that she didn't believe in handouts. Several others eyed me suspiciously. Judging by the fear in their white faces, the fact that I was, at that moment, a frantic, wild-eyed, Black teenager probably had something to do with it. But who had time to dispel racial stereotypes? The poetry raining down on me was slowing to a trickle. If I didn't find writing paper soon, the poem would be lost. (1998, 25)

For second person, the task would be harder, though not impossible. We could consider, for instance, this excerpt from Dorsey Seignious's "When You" from *You Are Here This Is Now*:

> When watching someone die, you must be very quiet. Always look down at the ground and examine your feet. Be uncomfortable and very somber. Allow your eyes to fill with tears. You will bite you lip until it bleeds, but you won't

notice until you wipe your tears with your sleeve and feel the sting of the sleeve on your lips. You will see the bloodstain on your sleeve, and then you will believe. (2002, 142)

Seignious's text demonstrates the sometimes unsettling quality of second person, as well as the intimacy of it. Or we could share "The Kid's Guide to Divorce," from *Self-Help*, by Lorrie Moore, which begins this way:

Put extra salt on the popcorn because your mom'll say that she needs it because the part where Inger Berman [*sic*] almost dies and the camera does tricks to elongate her torso sure gets her every time.

Think: Geeze, here she goes again with the Kleenexes.

She will say thanks honey when you come slowly, slowly around the corner in your slippers and robe, into the living room with Grandma's old used-to-be-salad-bowl piled high. I made it myself, remind her, and accidentally drop a few pieces on the floor. Mittens will bat them around with his paws.

Mmmmm, good to replenish those salts, she'll munch and smile soggily.

Tell her the school nurse said after a puberty movie once that salt is bad for people's hearts.

Phooey, she'll say. It just makes it thump, that's all. Thump, thump, thump—oh look! (1985, 49)

We imagine that we could then invite students to experiment and apprentice themselves to these mentor texts or others they might find, trying out different voices and points of view in order to get a feel for the effects and potential of each. Once we've tapped into the power of point of view, we could attempt to link that power to usage, so that students could have a real purpose and reason for making verbs and subjects agree. We could ask students to think of each sentence as a miniature story, in which there's a subject and a point of view that need to be aligned with a verb so as not to diminish the power and impact of the decisions and choices they made through avoidable, unnecessary errors.

We imagine it will take some trial and error before we get the scope and sequence of this inquiry, before we know where students will need scaffolding and where we will need to let them be, to learn and discover on their own. And we imagine that during this process we will frequently feel at sea, unsure if we will ever land on anything resembling solid ground. And so we take heart in

André Gide's words and hope that you will too, if you embark on an inquiry such as this or one you find in your heart.

And we take heart, as well, in Emerson's words, believing that what lies within is more important than what lies without. In terms of classrooms, what this means is that we believe it is less important to provide students with specific bits of knowledge than to make them want to possess and embrace knowledge because they see how it adds to the meaning and value of their lives. We want students to take what we give them and bring it into their hearts so that it can continue to empower and enrich them long after they leave us.

Similarly, we hope to empower teachers in the same way, so they are not dependent on us for texts and lesson plans, though we offer both freely as a place to start and a support to lean on. Thus, throughout this book we've tried to model what it means to read like a writer—or like a teacher of writing—in order to provide a vision of what it actually sounds and looks like, in the hope that readers will feel moved to think about texts in this way, too. As Julia Cameron writes, "the capacity for delight is the gift of paying attention." The more we pay attention, the more we delight—the more we find to delight in. And given the uncertain times that we suffer, we need to delight in language. And along with the challenges and the enduring work, we want to try to pass on that delight to fellow teachers—the delight of combing through bookshelves looking for texts, pulling out long-forgotten picture books we read to children now grown, and stumbling on Dayal Kaur Khalsa's *The Snow Cat*, for example, which draws us magically into the story with a series of evocative sentence fragments that are framed as rhetorical questions:

Have you ever lived alone at the edge of the woods in the middle of winter? When the snow is piled so high the eaves of the roof are a handspan away and you can break off icicles like crystal carrots? When endless, creamy fields of snow pour over the countryside, dolloping the horizon with little hills, already blurry again with new snow falling?

And the only sounds you hear are the howling wind at night and the whisper of fresh snow slithering against the windowpanes? Or, in the glistening day, you listen to the fairy tinkle of your snowshoes as you make long loops through the fields following rabbit tracks?

And the only face you ever see is your own, when, at the turn of the stairs each night you hold the candle aloft and catch a glimpse of yourself in the sleek back window, wavering like the moon fallen into a well? (1992, 1–3)

And we want to share the delight as well of opening a casually purchased novel, such as *Tourmaline*, by Joanna Scott, and being astonished by its opening paragraph:

Water laps against the quay of Portoferraio. Hungry dogs blink in the sunlight. A grocer stacks oranges. A carabiniere checks the time on his wristwatch. A girl chases a cat into a courtyard. Men argue in the shade of an archway. A woman rubs a rag over a shop window. Heels click on stone. Bottles rattle in the back of a flatbed truck. A boy writes graffiti on the wall above the steps leading to the Liceo Raffaello. German tourists hesitate before filing into a bar. An old woman, puzzled to find herself still alive at the end of the century, sits on a bench in Piazza Repubblica, her eyes closed, her lips moving in a silent prayer to San Niccolo. (2002, 3)

We delight in the way the text suddenly transports us to Italy, the way we see the girl chase the cat and hear the bottles rattle in the truck. And we delight as well as we suddenly realize what, grammatically, Scott has done: She has painted the scene with declarative sentences that seem to capture all the ease and simplicity of Italian life, sentences that seem to cast no shadow as if they had been forged and crafted under a bright Tuscan sun. Yet she ends with something more complex, more shaded: a sentence built of phrase upon phrase, like the sedimentary layers in which gemstones like tourmaline lie hidden, that hints at some mystery of place and time, of the weight of the centuries that you feel all around you when you're in such an ancient place.

Teachers of writing need to see language and imagine how to emulate it and how to teach its effects. As Saul Bellow says, "a writer is a reader who is moved to emulate." Thus as we read Joanna Scott, we, too, think about creating a scene through short, simple sentences that give way to something longer and more complex. And we finish Dayal Kaur Khalsa's book wanting to try our hand at a lead created through fragment questions. In his book on voice and style, Ben Yagoda also notes that a writer reads for *style*. "That, more than anything else," he writes, "is what separates the professionals from the civilians." He goes on to say:

When a reader fancies a particular author, it could be for any of a hundred reasons—the characters' names, the product placement, the political slant, the exotic locales, the sex scenes, the happy endings, the typeface on the dust jacket. But when one writer falls under another's spell, it is generally because of the way the [writer] uses language to forge or reflect an attitude toward the world—that is, it is because of style. (2004, 105)

We confess that we're obsessed with style, which we'll say, for the purposes of this book, is synonymous with, or so closely linked as to be synonymous with, voice. And we hope to pass on this obsession. We're convinced that readers are rarely immune to its spell, particularly if they are attending to what reactions a writer's words spark. Take this incident from a day spent recently at the Ohio Writing Project, working with Tom Romano and his graduate students in a class devoted to voice:

In addition to reading Tom's new book, *Crafting Authentic Voice* (2004), the class also looked at *Traveling Mercies*, by Anne Lamott (1999). While discussing the book, a middle school teacher said that she'd had an unusual experience with it the other day. She'd been reading it as she sat having coffee when she came to a particular passage in which Lamott describes an outing with her father and her brother to some tide pools by the beach. She was reading along, not especially engaged—not sure, in fact, that she liked the book or the author all that much—when something suddenly happened, and she found herself drawing back in her chair and holding the book farther away, as if to create a maximum distance between herself and the page. We asked her to show us the passage, and she directed us all to this page:

> We were, in fact, going to learn that afternoon that my father had a brain tumor on the word section of his brain, a metastasized melanoma, something no one had ever survived at that time. In just a week or so, doctors were going to take out as much as of the tumor as they could, but they weren't going to be able to get it all; its tentacles reached deep inside his brain . . . He was going to have the most aggressive forms of radiation and chemotherapy, be part of a clinical trial that wouldn't work for him; he was going to have one good year in between these treatments where he would be able to work off and on, and walk with us every day; he was going to live to see John graduate from Berkeley; he was going to live to see my younger brother graduate from high school; he was going to live to see me sell a novel about our family to a fancy

New York publisher. But then the cancer was going to start to eat away at his mind, and he was slowly going to end up like a huge friendly toddler . . . Maybe he would hear the music we played on the stereo in the cabin, maybe he would be aware of us watching him through the night, but what we did not know that day on the lava rock was that he was going to die two years from this August morning—this morning when the three of us were walking about peering into tide pools, with our dog Muldoon bumping into our legs, the late-summer diffusion of light making everything in the pools seem larger: the sea anemones, the bloom of the algae, the tiny crabs. (35)

Now, the death of a parent is always tragic for the children involved. And some people react in instinctual ways whenever the word *cancer* appears. But at the risk of sounding callous, we find that in a world full of misery, we often have to seal our hearts to other people's sorrow. We cannot always give ourselves to everyone's sad story, cannot always take on another's tragedy lest we find ourselves drained and depleted. Or sometimes the telling of the tragedy seems overly sentimental, as Yagoda remarks when he quotes Wilde: "One must have a heart of stone to read the death of Little Nell without laughing" (2004, xiii).

So we'd argue that it's not the subject alone that caused the teacher's reaction. There was something in the way it was told, in the way it was put together, with the repetition of *he was going; he was going* tolling like a death knell and propelling us inexorably toward a future that we could not escape or avoid. It is there in her word choice, there in her syntax, there in her punctuation: Lamott unleashes the power of grammar to staggeringly moving ends that are made even more so by setting these revelations against the idle world of the tide pools, where sea creatures sway and scuttle and drift, oblivious to the existence of death. And while it is perhaps presumptuous to assume that she did so with as much intention as we credit her for, it's hard not to imagine her writing the first sentence and then going on to the second, not fully aware of what she's created until, perhaps, the third, when suddenly the power of that phrase and that structure—the power inherent in the grammar—begins to dawn on her and she starts to manipulate it more consciously, repeating and honing and refining it further till it sings and bites like an axe.

Reading Lamott's text with a group of teachers helped us envision what would be common ways to use it as a mentor text and what would be new ways.

One of the most common ways to use such as text is as a topic springboard. We read a text that talks about friendship and we write about friendship, too. We see how writers write about their families and we understand that our families can be rich material for our writing, too. But frequently we stop there, not exploring what writers *do* with their topics and subjects, as if they are an end in themselves. Instead, as poet Diane Ackerman explains, "what it usually is is an occasion, catalyst, or tripwire that permits the [writer] to reach into herself and haul up whatever nugget of the human condition distracts her at the moment" (1991, 207).

One thing that helps us move away from content to a consideration of style is to look at one text, and then another, so that we see beyond content to the relationships of style and content. Another is to work at texts collaboratively with fellow readers. We looked next at "Around the Corner," by Sharon Bryan (1996), which appears in the anthology *In Short*, a marvelous collection of brief creative nonfiction, all one to five pages long:

> When I was small, maybe seven or eight, I noticed some crinkled leather boots in my mother's closet, some I knew I had never seen her wear. She told me they were for horseback riding, and showed me some funny-shaped pants. "They're called jodhpurs," she said, and spelled it for me. She said she'd ridden when she was in college. She had taken archery, too. She had planned to major in journalism so she could meet with world leaders, and she had interviewed the university president for the student newspaper. She had taken Spanish, and sometimes spoke phrases of it around the house: "You're *loco in la cabeza*," she would say to my father, and she had taught me to count from *uno* to *diez*. She also knew another language: shorthand. Her mother had made her take it because it was practical, and my mother had used it when she worked as a secretary at the truckline. She wrote her Christmas lists in shorthand—and anything else she didn't want me or my father to read, like her diary. It was a little red leather book with gilt-edged pages, and I was most intrigued by its little gold lock. As I remember it, my mother showed it to me, and maybe even read some passages to me. Looking over her shoulder I could see that some parts were in shorthand. When I asked what they said she just laughed and turned the page.
>
> My mother seemed to treat the diary—and the boots and jodhpurs, the glamorous pictures of herself that she had sent to my father overseas, her dreams of becoming a famous journalist—as relics of a distant past that no longer had much to do with her. She had left them all behind for life with my

father, and me, and eventually my two brothers. I loved my mother, and thought she was beautiful. I was grateful for the sort of mother she was—she had milk and cookies waiting when I came home from school, packed my lunchbox each morning. Every holiday was full of treats and surprises: a present by my plate on Valentine's Day, eggs hidden all over the house on Easter morning, Kool-Aid in my thermos on my birthday. Yet at the same time that I basked in the attention my mother lavished on me, I was haunted by the image of the person who seemed to have disappeared around the corner just before I arrived. (37)

The teachers who read this piece listed these possibilities for what it was about, in both big and small ways: the author's mother; the author's relationship with her mother; the inability to ever see one's parent as a completely separate person; the mystery of a parent's past; the mystery and fascination that some objects hold; the way that objects are a key to the past; dashed dreams; compromise; a daughter's ambivalent feelings about who she wants her mother to be—and perhaps who she wants to be herself; the changing role of women; a daughter's guilt; a mother's legacy. Some things in this list are clearly only content, but several are also about style and craft—the way the writer uses an object to suggest revelatory knowledge, the way the object juxtaposes areas of mystery with areas of understanding, the consistency of ambivalence.

Suddenly these two paragraphs seemed astoundingly rich, with the text operating on many different levels, and we envisioned a writing workshop where a standard conference question would be What nugget of the human condition are you exploring today? What mystery are you probing? Then we turned to look at how the piece was written to see what else we could learn, noting how the author used quotations both to capture the mother's personality and to alter the rhythm and sentence structure in order to make the piece lively, and how she used dashes to isolate what her mother kept private or hidden. Then another teacher spoke up. "I'm not quite sure I know how to say this," he began, "but it's as if she's laying it out for us so that we see the jodhpurs in the closet and the shorthand in the diary just as she did as a child, and we have to wait till the very last sentence to find out what these things really mean. And it kind of takes your breath away to realize that the piece is about so much more than just curiosity; it's as if the author turned a corner there, just as she thought her mother did." And it dawned upon us that the form of the piece was perfectly matched to the content, a realization we might not have arrived at had we not worked at the piece collectively, and had this teacher not tried to explain himself by pinning his feelings into language.

This gave us a richer appreciation for the artfulness of the piece, and we paused to reflect on how much would be lost if this material had been form-fitted into a five-paragraph essay. We envisioned it, though, easily enough:

1. *The Thesis Statement:* When I was a child I was fascinated by some of the things my mother kept from her college years, because they suggested that she'd been a different person than the mom I knew.

2. *Example 1:* The riding boots and jodhpurs

3. *Example 2:* The courses she took in college

4. *Example 3:* Her knowledge and use of shorthand

5. *The Conclusion:* Before my mother had me, she'd had an interesting life, and while I was glad that she stayed home with me, I sometimes wished that I could have known the person she was back then.

A piece written this way might manage to capture the ideas embedded in the original, but it would do so at the expense of the reader's engagement and the reader's pleasure at turning the final corner with the writer to see the mother's ghost hovering there, at the very edge of the page. It would demonstrate a certain lucid structure but would lose all its mystery and depth, the very things that make the piece so compelling.

And so we imagine that we will build on past work by continuing to talk about structure and voice and about how an audience can often determine the structure and voice that we use. We will talk about organization and focus, clarity and conciseness, but we will also talk about word choice and syntax, about rhythm, originality, and voice, providing our students with a grounding in grammar to ensure that they will be heard. And we imagine that there will be continued work to do here, and continuing challenges to face, among them convincing certain skeptical educators that all, not just some, of the students they teach have the potential to be more than functional writers. And this may, in turn, lead us to reexamine what we mean by functional or competent writing—

and may, in fact, necessitate reexploring what we mean when we say "to write."

Such explorations, however, are currently beyond the scope of this book. And so, in parting, we offer these words that we hope you take to heart: Be as fearless as André Gide's explorers setting sail for new lands. Trust that the answers you seek lie not with others but within you, as Emerson says. Let inequities of power and the oppression students experience outrage you and urge you to look outward. And seek out all the beauty that you can whenever you engage with words. Let commas make you swoon, let periods pierce your heart. And let sentences bring you satisfaction.

Usage Lessons

Beginning and Ending Punctuation

Writers capitalize the first letter of the first word of a sentence so the reader knows it is a new sentence. At the end of a sentence, we put ending punctuation (a period, an exclamation point, or a question mark). If we are writing by hand, then writers make an effort to be especially legible with capitals and ending punctuation so that readers recognize their sentences.

> In summer all the kids on our block played tackle tag. Chris, David, Billy, Karen, Michael, Ben, Amy, Lisa, and me. We played every night from right after supper until it was dark and we heard our mothers calling, whistling, or ringing bells.
>
> Sometimes we played in our backyard, where there was a treehouse to hide in and a garage to run around. But mostly we played on Mrs. Terhaar's lawn, where there was no place to get away, and the sidewalk, the street corner, and the driveway edged us in.

Writers make choices about ending punctuation to achieve certain effects. Ending punctuation choices include the period, the exclamation point, and the question mark.

A period achieves a neutral effect; it lets the reader create meaning from the words only.

> It made a difference if you were fast. [Implies: Hmm, OK, we'll learn more soon.]
> It made a difference to Chris. Chris was the fastest runner, and the most beautiful too.

An exclamation point implies a sense of overt excitement.

It made a difference if you were fast! [Implies: Wowza! You know what I mean!]

It made a difference to Chris! Chris was the fastest runner, and the most beautiful too!

A question mark implies a question or wonderment, bewilderment, or anxiety.

It made a difference if you were fast? [Implies: Why? Really? How? Are you sure?]

It made a difference to Chris? Chris was the fastest runner, and the most beautiful too?

Paragraphing

Writers break long chunks of writing into paragraphs. Writers often insert new paragraphs when

a new character enters a narrative

the setting changes

the time changes

someone new is speaking

the writer wants to introduce or emphasize a new idea

the writer wants to separate and emphasize different sections or subtopics

the writer wants to create a dramatic effect by isolating a sentence or chunk of sentences

The Parts of Speech

Noun: The name of a person, place, thing, idea (*summer, kids, block, tackle tag, lawn, street corner, driveway, Chris, hair, eyes, arms, legs, body, ground, something*)

Pronoun: A word that stands for a noun (*we, he, you, us, his, your*)

Verb: A word showing action or state of being (*played, run, knock, wrap, holding*)

Adjective: A word that describes or modifies a noun (*dark, fast, fastest, beautiful, yellow, blue, bare, brown, hard, undomesticated*)

Adverb: A word that describes or modifies a verb, an adjective, or an adverb (*most*)

The Sentence and the Fragment

A sentence includes a subject and a predicate. If the subject is *Chris*, the predicate is *what Chris does*. The subject can also include words that describe Chris. The predicate can also include words related to what Chris does. A sentence or clause always includes subject plus verb or verb phrase.

Subject: Chris   *Predicate:* **What Chris does**
(and how he is described)

Chris **was twelve.**
Chris **was truly heartbreakingly beautiful.**
Chris **was twelve and beautiful.**
Chris **was the fastest runner on our block.**
Chris **caught everyone when we played tackle tag.**
Chris, who was the fastest runner on our block, **caught everyone one
        night.**
Chris, who was twelve and beautiful, **caught everyone one night.**
Chris, who when he was twelve was the fastest runner and truly
        heartbreakingly beautiful, **caught everyone when we played
        tackle tag.**

Writers understand that a fragment is not a sentence. It doesn't have both a subject and a predicate. Fragments are used with an awareness of genre and audience. Writers understand that some audiences, such as academic publications and graders of standardized tests, are hostile to all fragments.

On the other hand, writers sometimes use fragments powerfully, to achieve a certain effect such as a rapid pace or an emphasis on detail. The last three sentences in this paragraph are not, in fact, full sentences; they are deliberate fragments:

> When Chris caught you in tackle tag, he lowered you to the ground gently, so that you lay in his hard arms for a minute, looking up at him through that tangle of yellow hair, the green lawn wet below you. Sticks in your back. Blue eyes laughing at you. Wild knowledge in your heart.

Subject, Verb, and Object Forms

Writers understand that if the subject is singular, so is the verb in the predicate. If the subject is plural, the verb in the predicate is plural too. That's why writers learn singular and plural forms of nouns, pronouns, and verbs.

> Only one girl was caught that time.
> All the girls were caught that time.

Some pronouns that we'd expect to be plural are singular. These include *each, either, every, everyone, everybody, neither, nobody, someone.*

> Every girl was caught that time.

Sometimes it is useful for writers to think about the idea of subject and object. In a sentence, the subject performs actions and the direct object receives action. The object is found in the sentence's predicate as in this sentence, where *Chris* is the subject, *Lisa* the direct object, and *caught Lisa first* the predicate.

> Chris caught Lisa first.

The subject can also have an indirect object (whom or what this action gets passed on to after the direct object). In this sentence, *Chris* is the subject, the *push* is the direct object, and *Lisa* is the indirect object.

> Chris gave Lisa a push.

Understanding subject and object helps us distinguish the proper forms of personal pronouns. Subject equals *I/you/he/she/we/they*. Object (direct or indirect) equals *me/you/him/her/us/them*.

I escaped Chris the first time, but just by a little.

    Chris chased Lisa and me. I wanted her to just disappear.

Prepositions, such as *to, for, in, under, above, toward,* and *in between,* link subjects and verbs to objects. And if the object is a personal pronoun, we use its object form (*me, you, him, her, us,* or *them*).

Chris ran toward us.

    Then Lisa ran in between Chris and me. She was a very fast runner.

Understanding subject and object helps us know when to use *who* and when to use *whom*.

Subject equals *who*.

Whoever slowed down, even for a moment, was in danger.

Object (direct or indirect or object of the preposition) equals *whom*.

He could catch whomever he wanted.

Verb Tense

Writers consider the tense in which they write, making choices about verb tense and maintaining verb forms consistent with those choices. Here are some ways writers consider verb tense:

Present tense often gives a sense of immediacy. It brings the reader into the story. It hints at a sense of things being unresolved. It can create tension, since the ending appears not yet experienced by the narrator. It implies a voice that is, in fact, writing from the age and events described in the piece. Present tense can be snappy and lively:

We play every night from right after supper until it is dark and we hear our mothers calling, whistling, or ringing bells. Sometimes we play in our backyard, where there is a treehouse to hide in and a garage to run around.

Past tense often creates a voice that is marked by a sense of reflection, by a looking back on events in order to see and understand more or in order to recover emotions or knowledge that has been buried. Past tense implies that the narrator has lived past these events and tells them now from an older vantage point. Past tense can be thoughtful and sometimes pensive. Past tense sometimes lets the narrator foreshadow events from a position of greater knowledge than the character has in the story:

> When Chris caught you in tackle tag, he lowered you to the ground gently, so that you lay in his arms for a minute, looking up at him through that tangle of yellow hair, the green lawn wet below you.

Sometimes writers change tense in order to change the mood. A shift from past to present tense can evoke a sudden shift in perspective or voice, from one that is contemplative or distant to one that is more animated, sometimes more dangerous or provocative:

> Chris's hair was yellow, his eyes were blue, his bare arms and legs were brown. When his hard sixth-grade arms wrap around your fourth-grade body, holding you just off the ground, it is like nothing you ever knew before. It is something undomesticated.

A shift to future tense evokes still another perspective, one that shows time passing and a future that may be known, dreamt, or dreaded:

> Mrs. Terhaar's lawn will lose its muddy spots where we slipped. The grass will turn gold, and then brown, and then we will say how cold it's gotten. We'll put on our school clothes, cover our legs and arms, watch our skin grow pale again.

Punctuating Dialogue

Writers who punctuate dialogue traditionally use quotation marks to indicate dialogue or direct speech. If the attribution—*he said* or *she said*—comes before the quoted speech, a comma is used after the *said,* and the dialogue terminates with ending punctuation that is inside the quotation marks. If the attribution appears after the quoted speech, a comma replaces the end punctuation. In either case we start the dialogue with a capital letter. In dialogue, each speech is usually a new paragraph, even if it is one word. This helps the reader figure out who is speaking.

The next time I let him catch me so that he would put his arms around me.
He said, "You're not running very fast tonight."
I said, "Really?"

Not all contemporary novelists follow this form anymore, but until one is a contemporary novelist, or sure of one's audience or purpose, it might be wise to.

The Faithful Comma: Lists, Conjunctions, Longer Sentences

Writers use commas to separate items in a list. The items can be nouns or actions.

Chris, David, Billy, Karen, Michael, Ben, Amy, Lisa, and me.
We heard our mothers calling, whistling, or ringing bells.

We can tuck items that go together in between the commas, and we can call attention to certain parts of the list by changing the order of the words:

Chris's hair was yellow, his eyes were blue, his bare arms and legs were brown.

When we join two complete sentences (both having a subject and a predicate) using the conjunctions *and, but, or, yet, so,* and *nor,* we use a comma.

Lisa had brown hair and slim legs. She was a very fast runner.
Lisa had brown hair and slim legs, and she was a very fast runner.

When we join a complete sentence (subject, predicate) with an incomplete sentence or clause (usually lacking a subject) using these conjunctions (*and, but, yet, so, nor*), we do *not* use a comma. Usually there's only one subject, so we don't want to separate that subject from the rest of the sentence.

Lisa had brown hair and slim legs and was a very fast runner.

Writers sometimes attach more description to the subject or predicate; if you can imagine this description in parentheses, then you enclose it commas. (These additions are called *parenthetic expressions.*) Follow your instincts or learn the complicated rules for clauses.

Chris (who was the fastest runner on our block) caught everyone when we played tag.

Chris, who was the fastest runner on our block, caught everyone when we played tag.

If the description is critical to the meaning of the sentence, then we don't enclose it in commas, so the reader understands that this description is no light matter. If the sentence below had commas around *in tackle tag,* the reader would wonder if the players were playing other tag games and if these other games also involved the players being knocked to the ground:

The tag in tackle tag consisted of being knocked to the ground.

Sometimes how we use commas indicates a slightly different meaning, as below. In the first sentence, only some girls experience Chris's arms in tackle tag.

The girls who were often caught by Chris glimpsed a hint of untamed experience.

In this sentence, all the girls get caught equally:

The girls, who were often caught by Chris, glimpsed a hint of untamed experience.

Now the boys can be caught, first some, and then all, and then some again:

The boys who were also caught by Chris must have felt something too.
The boys, who were also caught by Chris, must have felt something too.
Surely, the boys who were also caught by Chris must have felt something too.

Sometimes the use of commas is suggestive. This first example suggests that there is time for the narrator to take a breath between being caught and feeling those arms.

The next time I let him catch me, so that he would wrap his arms around me.

Everything happens very fast in the next example.

The next time I let him catch me so that he would wrap his arms around me.

We could slow it down even more, flirting, as it were, by putting in two commas:

The next time, I let him catch me, so that he would wrap his arms around me.

The Apostrophe

Apostrophes are used to show possession. To show possession, we follow these rules:

The apostrophe comes before the *s* with a singular noun and after the *s* with a plural noun.
Names ending in *s* still add an *'s* except for Jesus or those from antiquity.

Indefinite pronouns (*one, somebody, somebody else*) add *'s*, with the exception of *who* and *it*, which become *whose* and *its*.

An apostrophe is *not* used with personal pronouns (*mine, his, her, hers, your, yours, our, ours, their, theirs*).

Chris's blue gaze, his brown hands, set many girls' hearts beating
Some boys' hearts, undoubtedly, beat also for Chris, and his for theirs.
Jesus' disciples maybe felt like we did for Chris.
When he looked down at you, your heart's rhythm changed and the blood altered course in your veins.
He was like a young god, with his beauty that was like Achilles'.
Tackle tag often felt like the Trojan War, with all its jealousies and betrayals.

An apostrophe also marks time (perhaps thought of as possession of time).

In two week's time summer would end, and so would tackle tag on Mrs. Terhaar's lawn.

An apostrophe signifies contractions or missing letters. An apostrophe always marks the contraction of *it is* or *it has* to *it's*. (*Its* refers to possession.)

Mrs. Terhaar's lawn will lose its muddy spots where we slipped.
The grass will turn gold, and then brown, and then we will say how cold it's gotten.

Common contractions substitute an apostrophe for some of the letters in the following verbs: *is, are, will, would, not.* The apostrophe takes the place of all the letters except the last one or two in the substituted word. *We would* becomes *we'd. We will* becomes *we'll. We are* becomes *we're.*

> We'll put on our school clothes, cover our legs and arms, watch our skin grow pale again. At the elementary school, girls and boys have gym separately. Boys can't tackle girls and lower them gently to the ground. A girl in fourth grade and a boy in sixth grade won't glimpse each other slowing down.

An apostrophe always marks the contraction of *who is* or *who has* to *who's.*

> We won't hear any more those words, "Whose lawn should we use tonight?"
> Or, "Who's 'it'?"
> Or, "Chris is."

The Semicolon and the Colon

When we join two sentences using *however* or *nevertheless,* we use a semicolon rather than a comma.

> Lisa had been my best friend since kindergarten; nevertheless, I wanted her to disappear. I wanted the ground to open up and swallow her shiny hair and her white teeth and her long fast legs; however, that's not what happened.

The semicolon can create a feeling of suspense; there is more to know than what is stated in the first part.

> Chris admired kids who were fast; you could never just let him catch you. Whoever slowed down, even for a moment, was in danger; he could catch whomever he wanted.

The semicolon creates intimacy between two sentences that could stand on their own. It implies that one sentence is related closely to the other.

> Chris's hand was on her back; she stumbled and began to fall.

The colon introduces lists, particularly lists with large items, which we separate by semicolons.

This is what coursed through your blood when you felt Chris behind you: terror that you would be caught; dread that you would escape; and impatience to feel more.

The colon indicates clear causality.

Chris's hand was on her back: she stumbled and began to fall.

The colon introduces a significant question or statement.

When you felt Chris's arms around you, holding you just off the ground, you wondered: what would it feel like if this weren't tag?

The colon puts two statements together that define each other—the second one either explains the first or clearly denies it.

This I knew for sure: I would never miss a game of tackle tag if Chris were playing.
It was tag: it was something else entirely.

The Dash

The dash connects phrases and sentences. A dash is twice the length of the hyphen.

Tackle tag—these words still conjure magic.

The hyphen connects words. The hyphen is half the length of the dash.

I was a ten-year-old in the summer of fourth grade, and I would not feel a boy's arms around me like that again until I was seventeen.

Split Infinitives and Other Dangerous Liaisons

There is a misplaced notion that sentences must not begin or end with a preposition. Amis calls this idea "one of those fancied prohibitions (compare split infinitives) dear to ignorant snobs" (1997, 166).

To us he was like a god.

Amis says, "The idea that *and* must not begin a sentence, or even a paragraph, is an empty superstition. The same goes for *but*. Indeed either word can give unimprovably early warning of the sort of thing that is to follow" (14).

> To us he was like a god, with his beauty that was like Achilles'. And tackle tag often felt like the Trojan War, with all its jealousies and betrayals.

The rule against split infinitives, is, to quote Amis again, "the best known of the imaginary rules that petty linguistic tyrants seek to lay upon the English language. There is no grammatical reason whatever against splitting an infinitive and often the avoidance of one lands the writer in trouble" (218).

> A girl in fourth grade and a boy in sixth grade won't glimpse each other slowing down, waiting to be tenderly caught on a wet green lawn.

A Narrative of Conventions and Desire

Tackle Tag

In summer all the kids on our block played tackle tag. Chris, David, Billy, Karen, Michael, Ben, Amy, Lisa, and me. We played every night from right after supper until it was dark and we heard our mothers calling, whistling, or ringing bells. Sometimes we played in our backyard, where there was a treehouse to hide in and a garage to run around. But mostly we played on Mrs. Terhaar's lawn, where there was no place to get away, and the sidewalk, the street corner, and the driveway edged us in.

It made a difference if you were fast. It made a difference to Chris. Chris admired kids who were fast; you could never just let him catch you. Chris was the fastest runner, and the most beautiful too. Chris was often "it." Chris's hair was yellow, his eyes were blue, his bare arms and legs were brown. The tag in tackle tag consisted of being knocked to the ground. When his hard sixth-grade arms wrap around your fourth-grade body, holding you just off the ground, it is like nothing you ever knew before. It is something undomesticated.

Chris, who when he was twelve was the fastest runner and truly heartbreakingly beautiful, caught everyone when we played tackle tag. Whoever slowed down, even for a moment, was in danger; he could catch whomever he wanted. This is what coursed through your blood when you felt Chris behind you: terror that you would be caught; dread that you would escape; and impatience to feel more. When you felt Chris's arms around you, holding you just off the ground, you wondered: what would it feel like if this weren't tag? I escaped Chris the first time, but only by a little. Then Lisa ran in between Chris and me. Lisa had brown hair and slim legs and was a very fast runner. Chris caught Lisa first. Lisa had been my best friend since kindergarten; nevertheless, I wanted her to disappear. Chris's hand was on her back; she stumbled and began to fall. Only one girl was caught that time.

The next time I let him catch me so that he would put his arms around me.

He said, "You're not running very fast tonight."

I said, "Really?"

Chris's blue gaze and strong arms set many girls' hearts beating. The girls who were often caught by Chris glimpsed a hint of untamed experience. Surely, the boys who were also caught by Chris must have felt something too. Some boys' hearts, undoubtedly, beat also for Chris, and his for theirs. Jesus' disciples maybe felt like we did for Chris. When he looked down at you your heart's rhythm changed and the blood altered course in your veins. To us he was like a god, with his beauty that was like Achilles'. And tackle tag often felt like the Trojan War, with all its jealousies and betrayals. This I knew for sure: I would never miss a game of tackle tag if Chris were playing.

In two week's time summer would end, and so would tackle tag on Mrs. Terhaar's lawn. Mrs. Terhaar's lawn will lose its muddy spots where we slipped. The grass will turn gold, and then brown, and then we will say how cold it's gotten. We'll put on our school clothes, cover our legs and arms, watch our skin grow pale again. At the elementary school, girls and boys have gym separately. Boys can't tackle girls and lower them gently to the ground. A girl in fourth grade and a boy in sixth grade won't glimpse each other slowing down, waiting to be tenderly caught on a wet green lawn. We won't hear any more those words, "Whose lawn should we use tonight?"

Or, "Who's 'it'?"

Or, "Chris is."

Tackle tag—these words still conjure magic. I was ten years old in the summer of fourth grade, and I would not feel a boy's arms around me again like that until I was seventeen. It was tag: it was something else entirely. When Chris caught you in tackle tag, he lowered you to the ground gently, so that you lay in his arms for a minute, looking up at him through that tangle of yellow hair, the green lawn wet below you. Sticks in your back. Blue eyes laughing at you. Wild knowledge in your heart.

Acknowledgments

We are grateful to all the students and teachers who participated in this research, particularly the students and teachers of New York City, San Diego, Fort Worth, and southwestern Ohio. Some schools and teachers and administrators in New York City's District 2 were with us in this study over several years or for intense units of study, and they must be thanked by name: Jane Hsu and Clay Zwimmer at PS 116; Dan Feigelson and Alison Rini at PS 6; Alicia Perez and Carol Fan at Baruch College Campus High School; Karen Lowe, Matt Wayne, Teri Foley, and Val Assante at PS/IS 126; Ellen Foote, Donna Santman, Jenny Bender, and Audra Robb at IS 89 and Teachers College; and Sheri Donovan, Irma Medina, John Fanning, and Deborah Berg at PS/IS 111.

There are also some mentors whose work continues to challenge, provoke, and inspire us. We are thankful to Lucy Calkins not only for the personal example of her stamina and fervor but for the way she has believed generously in us and in the work and bestowed on us separately and together, over an almost twenty-year time span, diverse and fertile opportunities to study reading and writing in communities committed to improving practice.

We are endlessly grateful to Maureen Barbieri, whose real love and knowledge of writing and graceful but entirely firm resistance to dogma continue to steer us. Maureen raises her eyebrows at clichés, glows when words sparkle for her, is always ready with a glass of wine and a new book of poetry. Maureen is a muse.

Tom Romano, too, has been a mentor. Tom's spirited defense of originality over banal conformity in writing has helped us through many dark nights of the soul. It was Tom's early work that led us into high school English classrooms, his multigenre work that helped us pay more attention to form, and his recent work on voice that stimulated us to hold dearly and tenaciously to this endangered quality.

We began this work under the aegis of Shelley Harwayne and Andrea Lowenkopf, both of whom offered us invaluable opportunities to pursue the work and share it at various stages with principals and staff developers throughout Manhattan's District 2. We also have to thank Shelley more generally for her contagious joy in children and their writing, which has kept so many teachers in the field, and for always keeping her sights on the true goals of literacy.

We also engaged in much of this work under the auspices of Diane Snowball's organization, AUSSIE, and we thank both Diane and our American and Australian colleagues for the support, the interest, and the wonderful camaraderie they offered us over the years.

And then there are our families and those dearest colleagues whose warmth, ardor, and humor sustain us in all our endeavors. Thank you to Debora St. Claire for listening so carefully to this and all our stories. Thank you to Dorothy Barnhouse for your wise words and unwavering friendship. Thank you to Kay Lohnes for the days and years of loving support, to Jackson Ehrenworth for four years of joy, and to Michela Vinton for the constant delight and meaning you bring to life.

And, finally, to Andrew Ehrenworth, who found the Nabokov sentence that started it all, who put down paintbrush to ponder clauses, who settled the sleepless child and questions of semicolons, both thankfulness and enduring love.

Bibliography

ACKERMAN, DIANE. 1991. "White Lanterns." In *The Writer on Her Work*, ed. Janet Sternburg, Vol. 2, 201–09. New York: W. W. Norton.

AMIS, KINGSLEY. 1997. *The King's English: A Guide to Modern Usage*. New York: St. Martin's Griffin.

ANGELILLO, JANET. 2002. *A Fresh Approach to Teaching Punctuation*. New York: Scholastic.

ATWELL, NANCIE. 1998. *In the Middle: New Understandings About Writing, Reading and Learning*. Portsmouth, NH: Heinemann.

BARBIERI, MAUREEN. 1995. *Sounds from the Heart: Learning to Listen to Girls*. Portsmouth, NH: Heinemann.

———. 2002. *Change My Life Forever: Giving Voice to English Language Learners*. Portsmouth, NH: Heinemann.

BRYAN, SHARON. 1996. "Around the Corner." In *In Short*, ed. Judith Kitchen and Mary Paumier Jones, 37–38. New York: W. W. Norton.

CALKINS, LUCY. 1996. *The Art of Teaching Writing*. Portsmouth, NH: Heinemann.

CALKINS, LUCY, AND TEACHERS COLLEGE READING AND WRITING PROJECT. 2003. *Units of Study for Primary Writing*. Portsmouth, NH: Firsthand.

CHABON, MICHAEL. 2000. *The Adventures of Kavalier and Clay*. New York: Picador.

CHEUSE, ALAN. 2003. "Starting Late." In *Writers on Writing II: More Collected Essays from the New York Times*, ed. Will Shortz, 25–30. New York: Times Books.

CISNEROS, SANDRA. 1991a. *Woman Hollering Creek*. New York: Random House.

———. 1991b. *Woman Hollering Creek and Other Stories*. New York: Vintage.

COLLINS, BILLY. 1998. *Picnic, Lightning*. Pittsburgh: University of Pittsburgh Press.

CORIMER, ROBERT. [1977] 1997. *I Am the Cheese*. New York: Knopf.

CURRIE, MARK. 1998. *Postmodern Narrative Theory*. London: Palgrave.

DAHL, ROALD. [1961] 1996. *James and the Giant Peach*. New York: Alfred Knopf.

DELPIT, LISA. 1995. *Other People's Children: Cultural Conflict in the Classroom*. New York: New.

DEWEY, JOHN. [1900] 1990. *The School and Society*. Chicago: University of Chicago Press.

———. [1916] 1944. *Democracy and Education: An Introduction to the Philosophy of Education*. New York: Free.

DILLARD, ANNIE. 1989. *The Writing Life*. New York: Harper and Row.

DOCTOROW, E. L. 1982. *Loon Lake*. New York: Random House.

EGAN, KIERAN. 1990. *Romantic Understanding: The Development of Rationality and Imagination, Ages 8–15*. New York: Routledge.

———. 1992. *Imagination in Teaching and Learning: The Middle School Years*. Chicago: University of Chicago Press.

EHRENWORTH, MARY. 2003. *Looking to Write*. Portsmouth, NH: Heinemann.

FLEISCHMAN, PAUL. 1991. *The Borning Room*. New York: Harper Collins.

FOWLER, H. W., and F. G. FOWLER. [1906] 2002. *The King's English*. Oxford: Oxford University Press.

FRITZ, JEAN. 1982. *Homesick: My Own Story*. New York: Putnam.

GARDNER, JOHN. 1984. *The Art of Fiction*. New York: Alfred A. Knopf.

GREENE, MAXINE. 1995. *Releasing the Imagination: Essays on Education, the Arts, and Social Change*. San Francisco: Jossey-Bass.

———. 2000. "Imagining Futures: The Public School and Possibility." *Journal of Curriculum Studies* 32: 267–80.

GRIMES, NIKKI. 1998. *Jazmin's Notebook*. New York: Dial.

HARWAYNE, SHELLEY. 2001. *Writing Through Childhood: Rethinking Process and Product*. Portsmouth, NH: Heinemann.

———, ed. 2002. *Messages from Ground Zero*. Portsmouth, NH: Heinemann.

HEARD, GEORGIA. 1989. *For the Good of the Earth and Sun: Teaching Poetry*. Portsmouth, NH: Heinemann.

———. 1998. *Awakening the Heart: Exploring Poetry in Elementary and Middle School*. Portsmouth, NH: Heinemann.

———. 2002. *The Revision Toolbox: Teaching Techniques That Work*. Portsmouth, NH: Heinemann.

HESHUSIUS, LOUS. 1989. "The Newtonian Mechanistic Paradigm, Special Education, and the Contours of Alternatives: An Overview." *Journal of Learning Disabilities* 22: 402–15.

HOOKS, BELL. 1994. *Teaching to Transgress: Education as the Practice of Freedom*. New York: Routledge.

IYER, PICO. 1996. "In Praise of the Humble Comma." In *In Short*, ed. Judith Kitchen and Mary Paumier Jones, 78–82. New York: W. W. Norton.

Jaeggy, Fleur. 1989. *Sweet Days of Discipline*. New York: New Directions.

Khalsa, Dayal Kaur. 1992. *The Snow Cat*. New York: Clarkson Potter.

Ladson-Billings, Gloria. 1994. *The Dreamkeepers: Successful Teachers of African American Children*. San Francisco: Jossey-Bass.

Lamott, Anne. 1994. *Bird by Bird*. New York: Pantheon.

———. 1999. *Traveling Mercies: Some Thoughts on Faith*. New York: Random House.

Lattimer, Heather. 2003. *Thinking Through Genre: Units of Study in Writing Workshop 4–12*. Portland, ME: Stenhouse.

Lederer, Richard. 1987. *Anguished English*. New York: Dell.

Marcus, Leonard S. 2000. *Author Talk*. New York: Simon and Schuster.

Marquart, Deborah. 1998. "Getting Ready." In *Welcome to Your Life: Writings for the Heart of Young America*, ed. David Haynes and Julie Landsman, 63. Minneapolis: Milkweed.

Miller, Laura. 2004. "Divorce That Book." *New York Times Review of Books* 9 May.

Moore, Lorrie. 1985. *Self-Help*. New York: Knopf.

Morrison, Toni. 1993. *Playing in the Dark: Whiteness and the Literary Imagination*. New York: Vintage.

Murdoch, Iris. 2001. *The Sovereignty of Good over Other Concepts*. New York: Routledge.

Murray, Donald. 1985. *A Writer Teaches Writing*. Portsmouth, NH: Heinemann.

———. 1990. *Shoptalk: Learning to Write with Writers*. Portsmouth, NH: Boynton/Cook.

———. 1997. *The Craft of Revision*. New York: Harcourt Brace.

Myers, Walter Dean. 1998. "The Escape." In *Trapped: Cages of Mind and Body*, ed. Lois Duncan, 101–14. New York: Simon and Schuster.

Nabokov, Vladimir. 1989. *Lolita*. New York: Vintage.

Noden, Harry. 1999. *Image Grammar*. Portsmouth, NH: Heinemann.

Noguera, Pedro. 2003. *City Schools and the American Dream: Reclaiming the Promise of Public Education*. New York: Teachers College Press.

Potok, Chaim. 1998. *Zebra and Other Stories*. New York: Knopf.

Rodriguez, W. R. 1998. "justice." In *Welcome to Your Life: Writings for the Heart of Young America*, ed. David Haynes and Julie Landsman, 78. Minneapolis: Milkweed.

Romano, Tom. 1995. *Writing with Passion*. Portsmouth, NH: Heinemann.

———. 1999. *Blending Genres, Altering Styles*. Portsmouth, NH: Heinemann.

———. 2004. *Crafting Authentic Voice*. Portsmouth, NH: Heinemann.

ROSENTHAL, JOHN. 2004. "The Elements of Common Sense." *The New York Times* 3 May.

SAPPHIRE, RAMONA. 1997. *Push*. New York: Random House.

SARAMAGO, JOSE. 1998. *The Tale of the Unknown Island*. New York: Harcourt.

SCHINE, CATHLEEN. 1995. *The Love Letter*. New York: Plume.

SCHOLES, ROBERT. 1989. *Protocols of Reading*. New Haven, CT: Yale University Press.

SCHUSTER, EDGAR. 2003. *Breaking the Rules: Liberating Writers Through Innovation*. Portsmouth, NH: Heinemann.

SCOTT, JOANNA. 2002. *Tourmaline*. New York: Little, Brown.

SEARS, VICKI. 1997. "Dancer." In *Leaving Home*, ed. Hazel Rochman, 21–25. New York: Harper Collins.

SEDGWICK, EVE KOSOFSKY. 1990. *Epistemology of the Closet*. Berkeley: University of California Press.

SEIGNIOUS, DORSEY. 2002. "When You." In *You Are Here This Is Now*, ed. David Levithan, 142–43. New York: Scholastic.

SNOWBALL, DIANE, and FAYE BOLTON. 1999. *Spelling K–8: Planning and Teaching*. Portland, ME: Stenhouse.

SPUFFORD, FRANCIS. 2002. *The Child That Books Built*. New York: Picador.

STEIG, WILLIAM. 1971. *Amos and Boris*. New York: Farrar, Straus, and Giroux.

———. 1986. *Brave Irene*. New York: Farrar, Straus, and Giroux.

STEIN, GERTRUDE. 1967. *Look at Me Now and Here I Am: Writings and Lectures 1909–45*. Baltimore: Penguin.

STRUNK, WILLIAM, and E. B. WHITE. 2000. *The Elements of Style*. New York: Longman.

THOMPSON, AUDREY. 1998. "Not the Color Purple: Black Feminist Lessons for Educational Caring." *Harvard Educational Review* 68: 522–54.

THURBER, JAMES. 2001. *The Years with Ross*. New York: Harper Collins.

TRUSS, LYNNE. 2003. *Eats, Shoots and Leaves*. New York: Gotham.

WALKER, ALICE. 1990. *The Color Purple*. New York: Simon and Schuster.

WEAVER, CONSTANCE. 1996. *Teaching Grammar in Context*. Portsmouth, NH: Heinemann.

———. 1998. *Lessons to Share on Teaching Grammar in Context*. Portsmouth, NH: Heinemann.

WELTY, EUDORA. 1983. *One Writer's Beginnings*. Cambridge, MA: Harvard University Press.

WHITE, E. B. [1945] 1973. *Stuart Little*. New York: Harper Collins.

WOLFE, TOM. 1979. *The Right Stuff*. New York: Farrar, Straus, and Giroux.

WOOD RAY, KATIE. 2002. *What You Know by Heart: How to Develop Curriculum for Your Writing Workshop*. Portsmouth, NH: Heinemann.

WOODSON, JACQUELINE. 1995. *From the Notebooks of Melanin Sun*. New York: Scholastic.

YAGODA, BEN. 2004. *The Sound on the Page: Style and Voice in Writing*. New York: Harper Collins.

ZOLOTOW, CHARLOTTE. 1972. *William's Doll*. New York: Harper Collins.

Index

semicolons (*cont.*)
   creating suspense with, 79–80,
      180
   curriculum calendar, 45
   joining sentences with, 72, 79,
      180
   using, 79–80, 180–81
sentence-level writing, 129–58
   apprenticeships, 129–36
   collaborative, 143–46
   creating scenes with, 164–65
   examining mentor text on charts,
      135
   list sentences, 146–49
   mentor texts for, 130–34
   parts of speech in, 141
   peer writing response to, 145–46
   reading sentences closely, 136–39
   student engagement with, 137
   turning sentences into poems,
      138–39, 149
   voice in, 132–34
sentences
   beginning or ending with
      prepositions, 82–83
   breaking into more than one, 34
   capitalizing first word of, 21, 23,
      58, 171
   charting, 140–44
   "clipped," 63
   combining, 151–53
   commas and, 38–39, 71–76, 177
   connecting with dashes, 81–82
   diagramming, 40, 49, 140
   as emotional, 61
   emulation of, 38
   fragments, 63–64
   guidelines for writing, 173–74
   joining with commas, 71–73, 177
   joining with semicolons, 79, 180
   mentor, 150–51
   noticing, 37–38
   predicates in, 62
   revision, 46–47
   rhythm in, 84, 141
   satisfaction in writing, 89
   subjects of, 62
   varying structure of, 152
   wordy, 119–22
serial commas, 3

"Silenced Dialogue, The" (Delpit),
   50
Snowball, Diane, 19
Snow Cat, The (Khalsa), 163
Soto, Gary, 129
*Sound on the Page, The: Style and
   Voice* (Yagoda), 5, 128–29, 136,
   152
Spelling K–8 (Snowball and Bolton),
   31
split infinitives, 3, 82–84, 181–82
Spufford, Francis, 12
Stafford, William, 1
standardized tests, voice and, 9
statements, introducing with
   colons, 80–81
Steig, William, 129, 137, 138, 139,
   143, 145, 146–47, 151, 156,
   157
Stein, Gertrude, 49, 61, 70, 159
stories
   embedding lessons in, 22, 28
   emotional truth in, 56–57
   fictionalizing, 56–57
   grammar instruction and,
      53–58
   learning from, 12–13
   minilessons using, 55–56
   power of, 53–54
   romance in, 57
   sources of, 56
   unsafe, 54–55
strategic plans, 15–16
Strunk, William, 5, 7, 53, 60, 63, 64,
   66, 73, 84
Stuart Little (White), 120, 121, 127,
   148–49, 150–51, 157, 158
style
   commas and, 75–76
   reading for, 164–65
style manuals, 5
subject and object
   curriculum calendar, 44, 45
   guidelines for, 174–75
   subject-verb agreement and,
      65–67
subjects. *See also* nouns
   curriculum calendar, 44, 45
   parenthetic expressions about,
      177–78

related words after, 63
   sentences and, 62–63
subject-verb agreement, 64–67
   curriculum calendar, 44, 45
   point of view and, 160
suspense, creating with semicolons,
   79–80, 180
Sweet Days of Discipline (Jaeggy),
   127–28, 155, 158
syllabic count, 145

"Tackle Tag," 84–86, 183–84
teachers
   concerns about grammar, 15,
      49–50
   outward-looking quality of,
      159–60
   role in grammar instruction,
      52–53
Teachers College Reading and
   Writing Project, 15
Teaching Grammar in Context
   (Weaver), 19, 53
teaching points, 22
Teaching to Transgress (hooks), 13
tension
   creating, 145
   dialogue and, 70
   present tense and, 175
   verb tense and, 68
Thinking Through Genre (Lattimer),
   16
third person, 160
Thompson, Audrey, 12–13
Thurber, James, 75–76
time passage
   apostrophes and, 77, 179
   verb tense and, 68
titles, 94
tone
   ending punctuation and, 60
   establishing, 20–22
   reading for, 139–46
   verb tense and, 67
Tourmaline (Scott), 164
Traveling Mercies (Lamott), 165–66
Truss, Lynne, 2–3, 49, 53, 54, 70,
   76
truth, of story examples, 56–57
Tuchman, Barbara, 89

undefined pronouns, 66
units of study
    curriculum planning and, 16
    on drafting, 29
    on freewriting, 29
    planning, 16, 104–5
    on revision, 29
    rule-breaking experimentation,
        101–5
unpunctuated writing
    apprenticeship, 95–101
    guidelines for using, 95
    inquiry, 90–94
    mentor texts, 90–92, 98
    unit planning, 101–6
unsafe stories, 54–55

verbal skills, original thinking and,
    88
verbs. *See also* predicates
    defined, 62, 172
    guidelines for, 174–75
verb tense, 67–69
    curriculum calendar, 45
    guidelines for, 175–76
    mood and, 68, 176
    past tense, 67–69, 154, 155,
        175–76
    present tense, 67–69, 154, 155,
        175
    shifting, 153–54
    tone and, 67
    uses of, 67–69

voice
    adolescence and, 9
    collective, 143–46
    commas and, 75–76
    cultural diversity and, 51–52
    defined, 8
    fragments and, 118
    grammatical usage and, 52
    importance of, 8–10
    mimicking, 39
    rule-breaking and, 99–100,
        101–2, 112, 125–26
    in sentence-level writing,
        132–34, 149
    standardized tests and, 9
    verb tense and, 69, 175

Walker, Alice, 70
Weaver, Constance, 19, 53, 65, 84
Welcome to Your Life (Haynes and
    Landsman), 90–92, 112–13
Welty, Eudora, 58
Wharton, Edith, 128
What You Know by Heart (Ray), 16
"When You" (Seignious), 161–62
White, E. B., 5, 7, 53, 58, 60, 63, 64,
    66, 73, 78, 84, 120, 121, 127,
    129, 148, 150–51, 157–58
who/whom, 66–67, 175
who/who's, 180
Wilde, Oscar, 166
William's Doll (Zolotow), 119
Wolfe, Tom, 120, 121

Woman Hollering Creek (Cisneros),
    150, 153–54
Woodson, Jacqueline, 116, 118
word choice, 21
word play, 52, 89, 149
wordy sentences, 119–22
    guidelines for using, 121–22
    mentor texts for, 119–21
Writer Teaches Writing, A (Murray),
    16–17
writing instruction, 7
writing process
    culture of power and, 4, 50–51
    defined, 16–17
    grammar and, 37
    teaching and, 16–17
writing workshop
    curriculum calendar for, 16–17
    teaching conventions in, 18–19

Yagoda, Ben, 5, 128–29, 132, 136,
    152, 164
Years with Ross, The (Thurber),
    75–76
You Are Here This Is Now, 161–62

Zebra and Other Stories (Potok), 33
Zolotow, Charlotte, 119
Zolotow, Charlotte, Award, 119